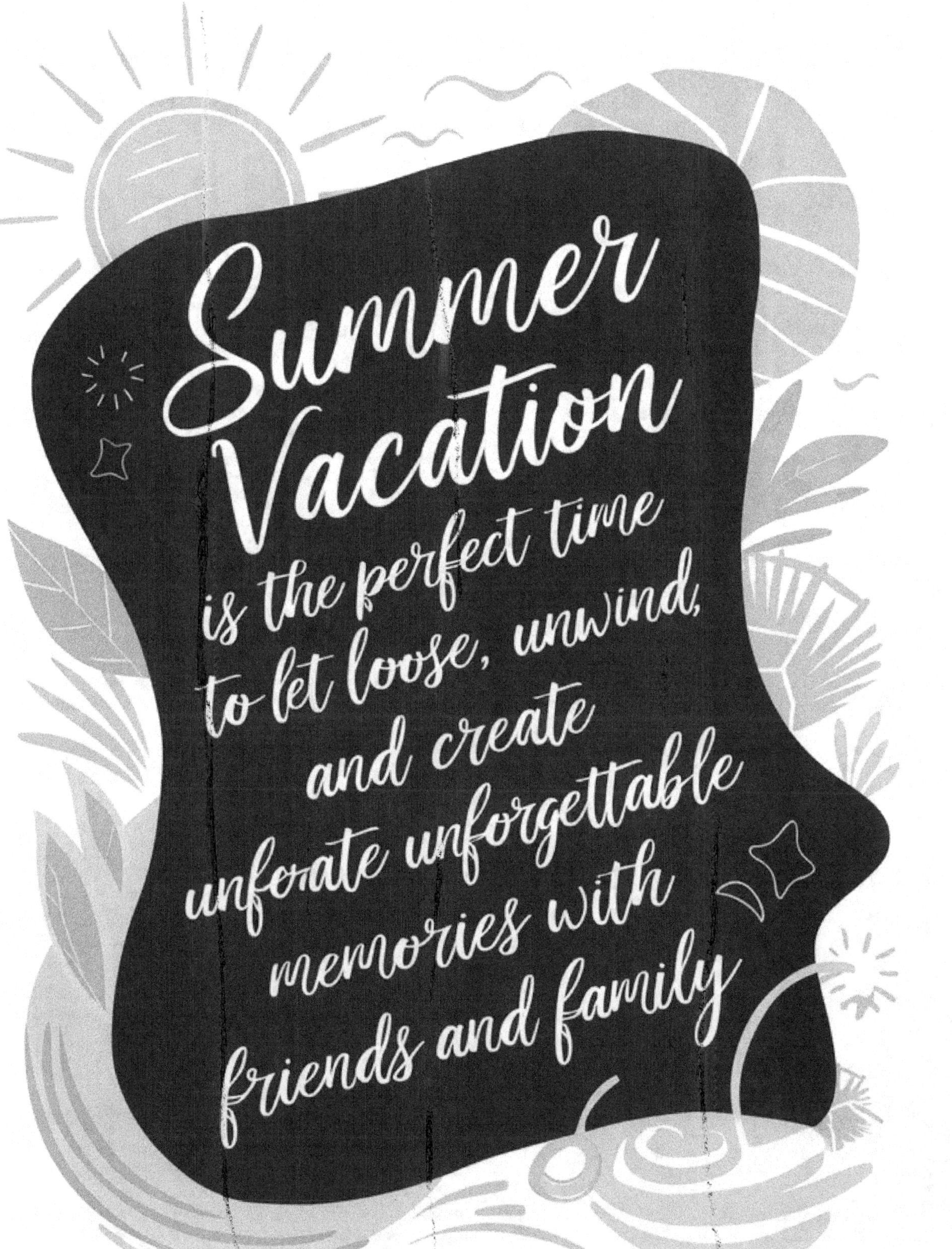
Summer
Vacation
is the perfect time
to let loose, unwind,
and create
unforate unforgettable
memories with
friends and family

coloring book for Adult & kids

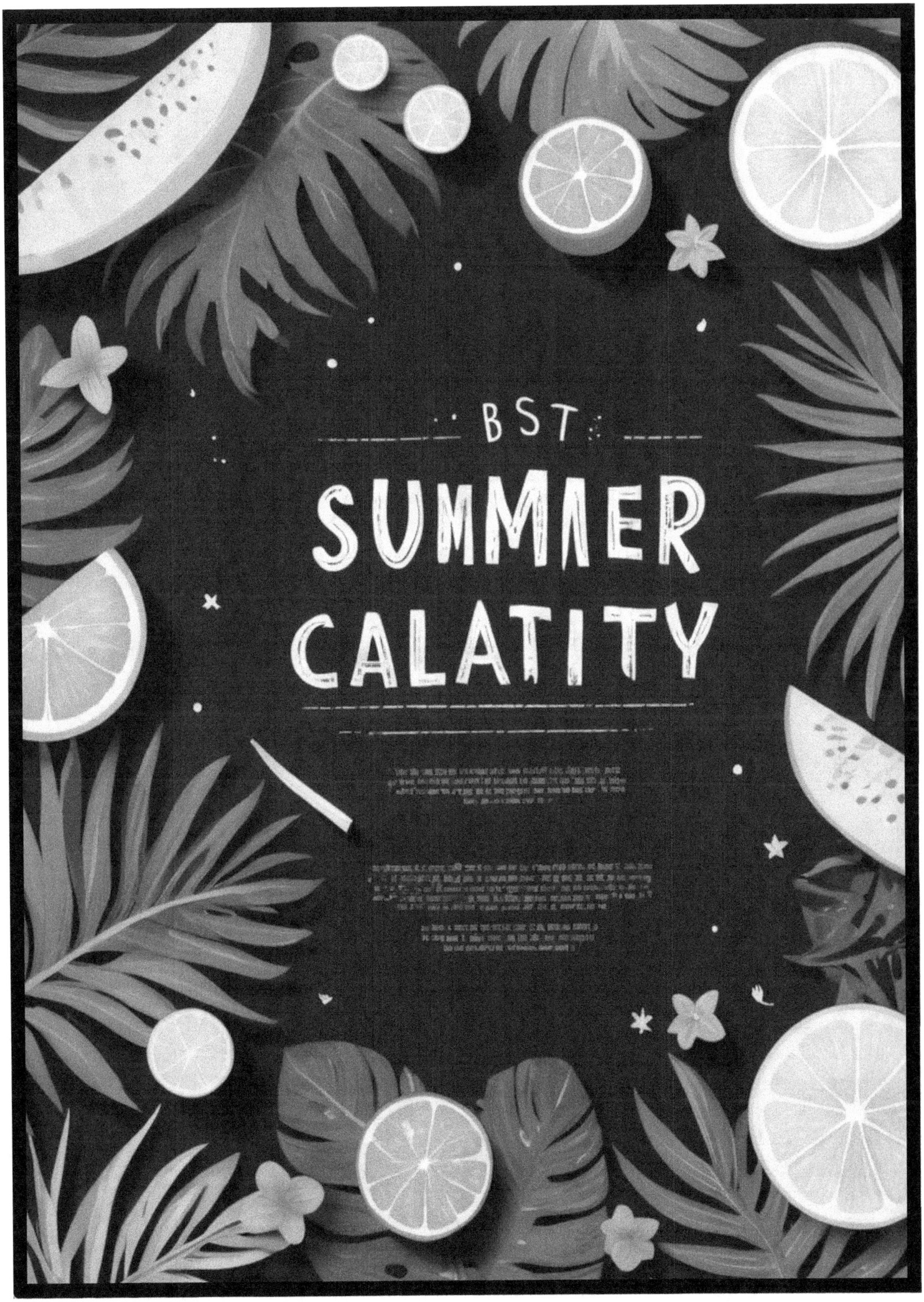
BST
SUMMIER
CALATITY

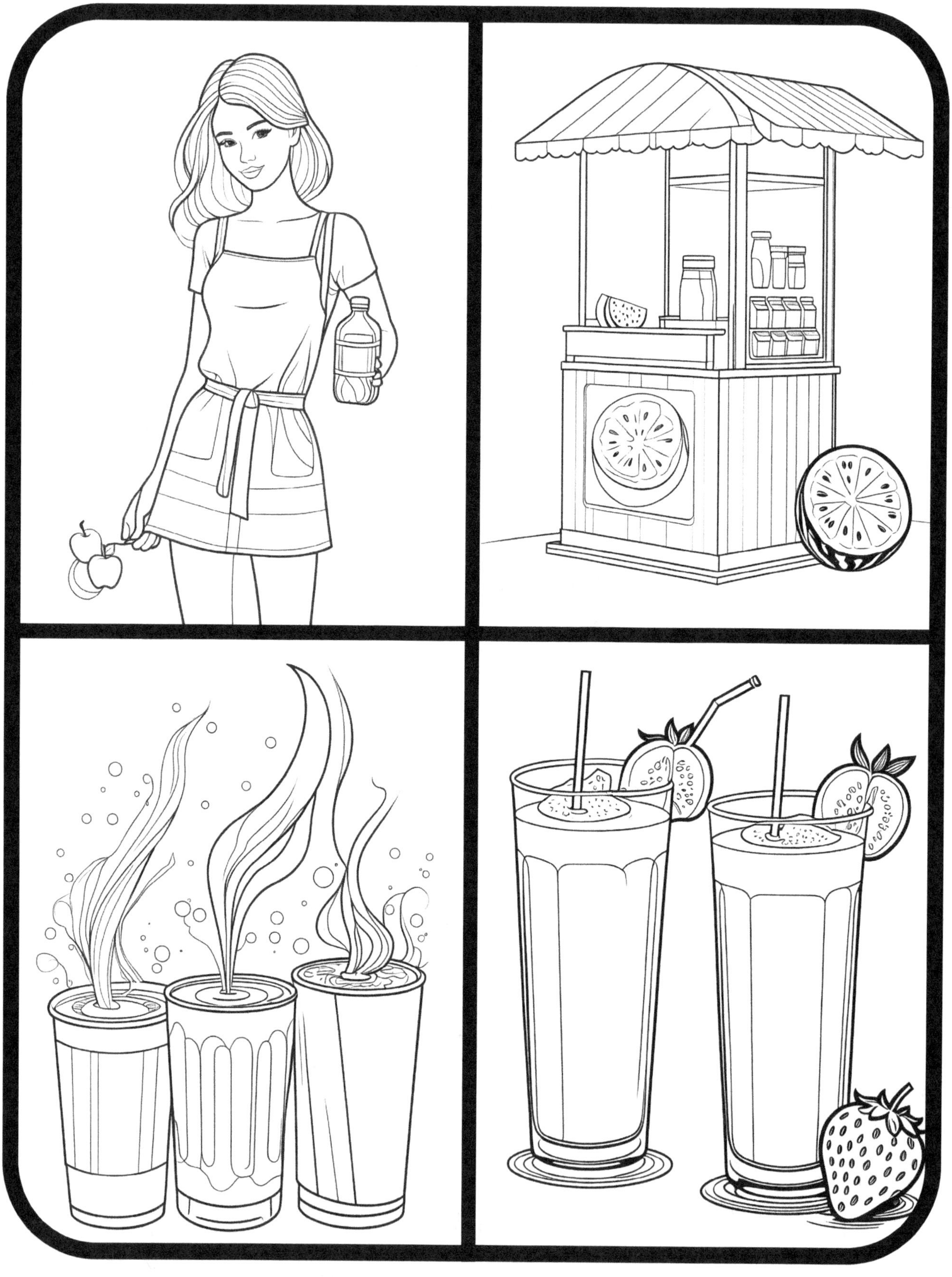

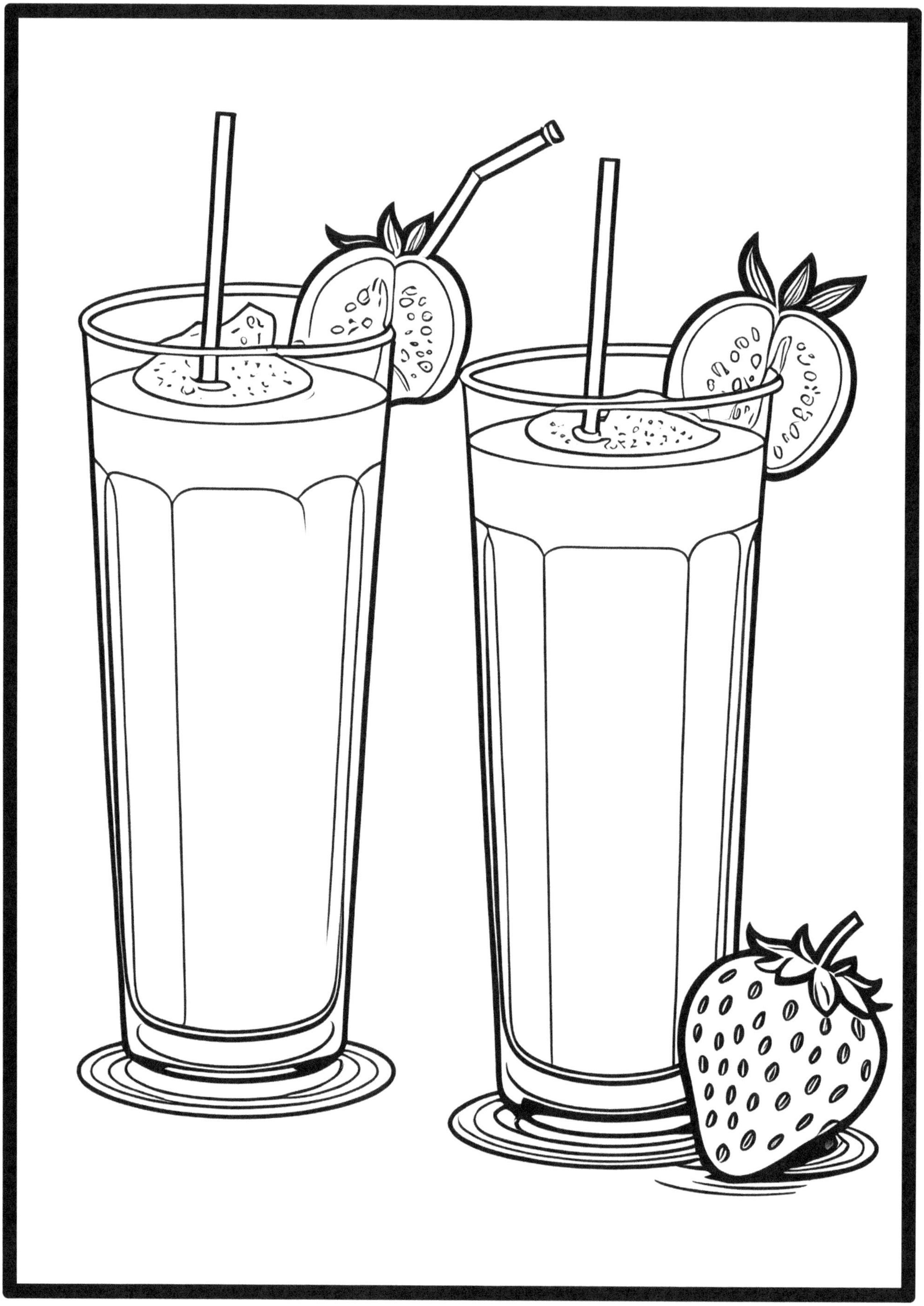

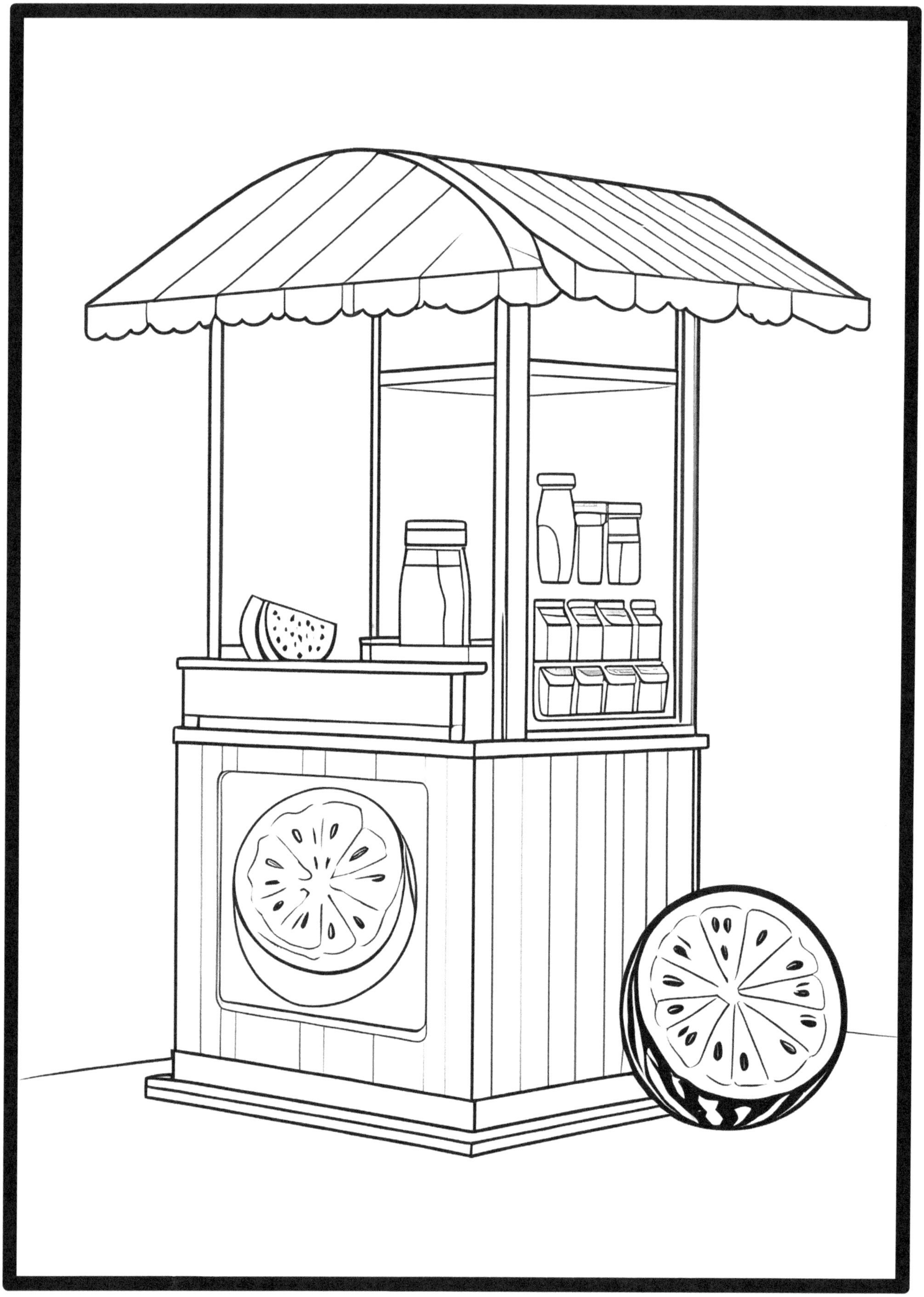

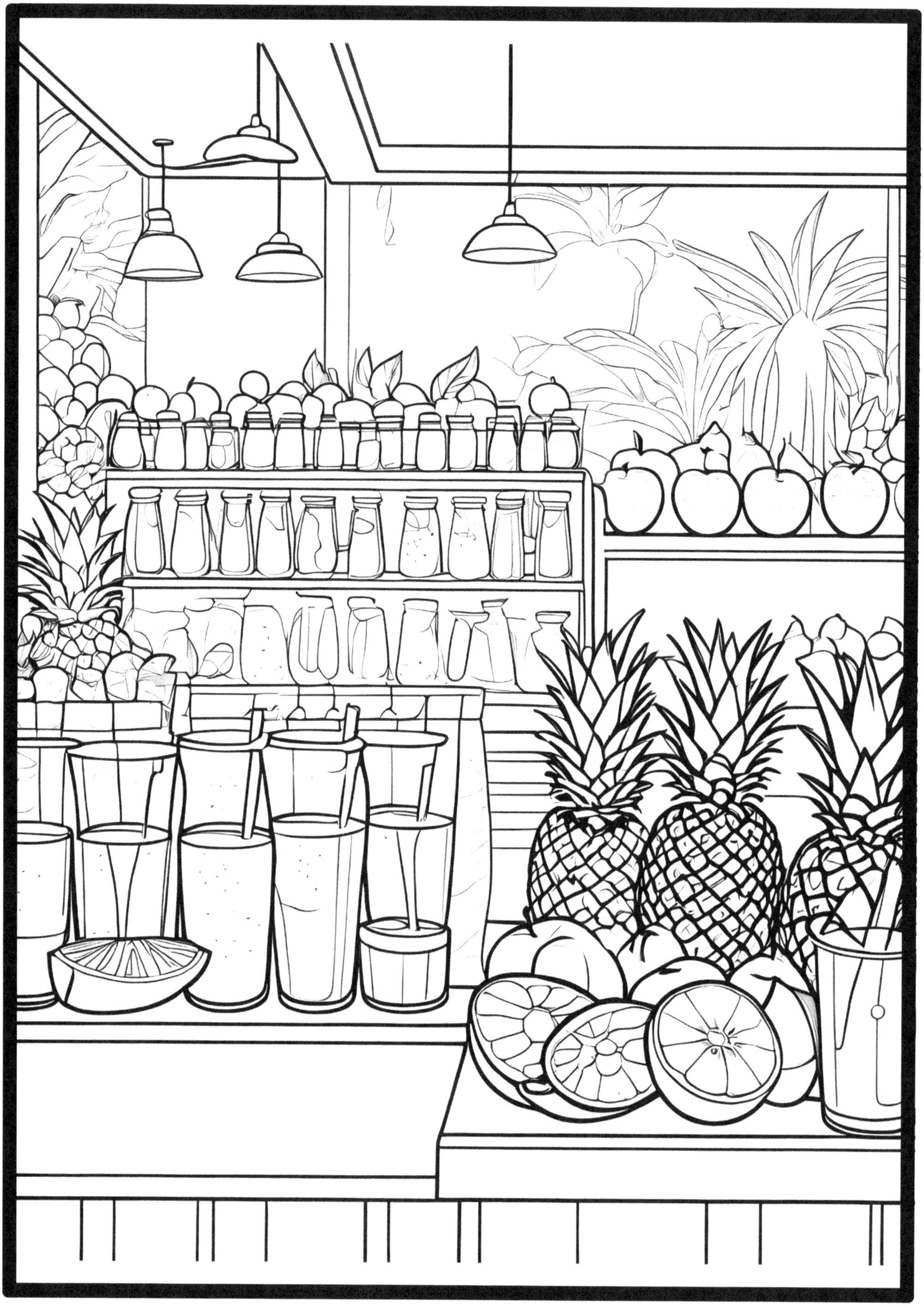

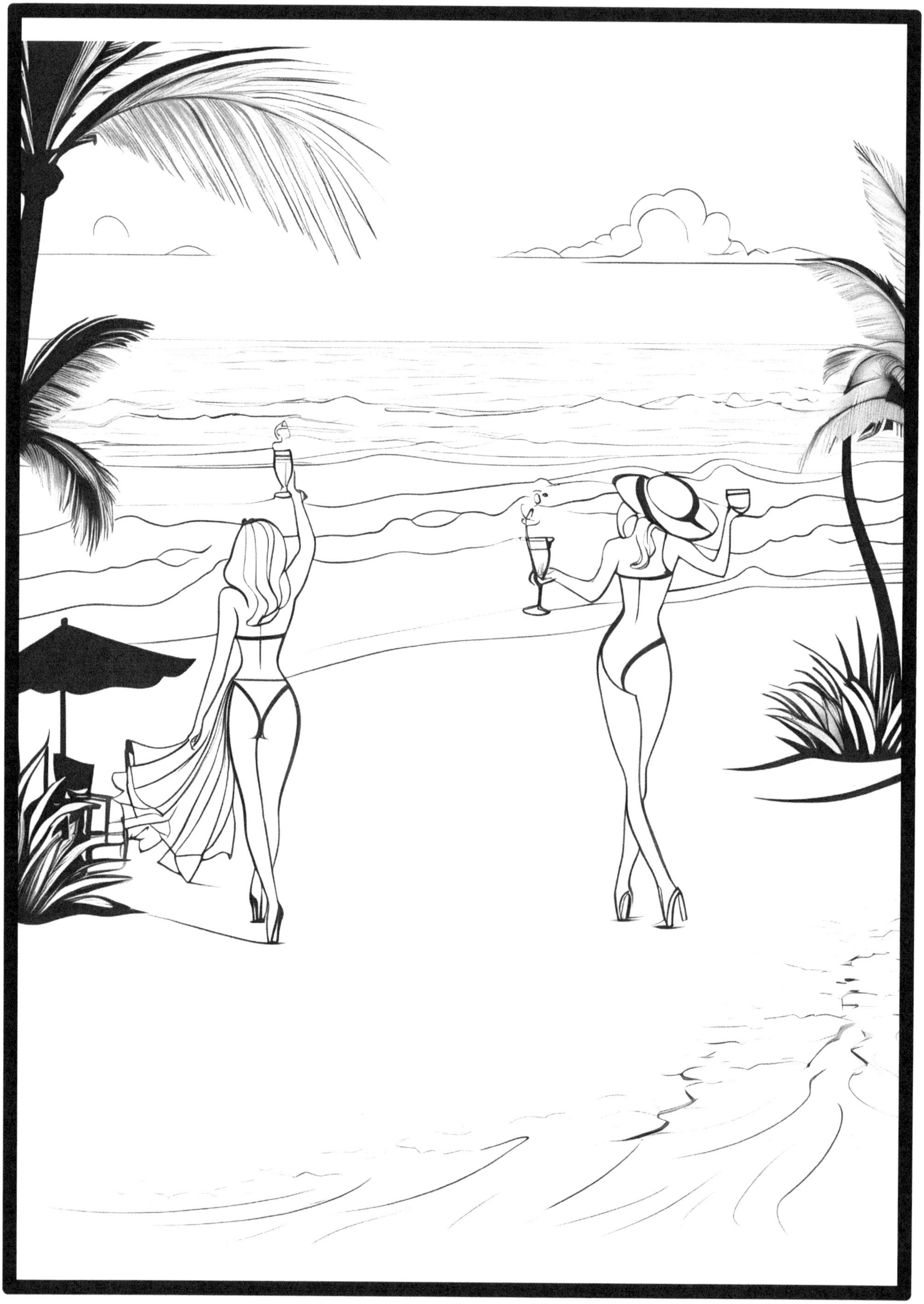

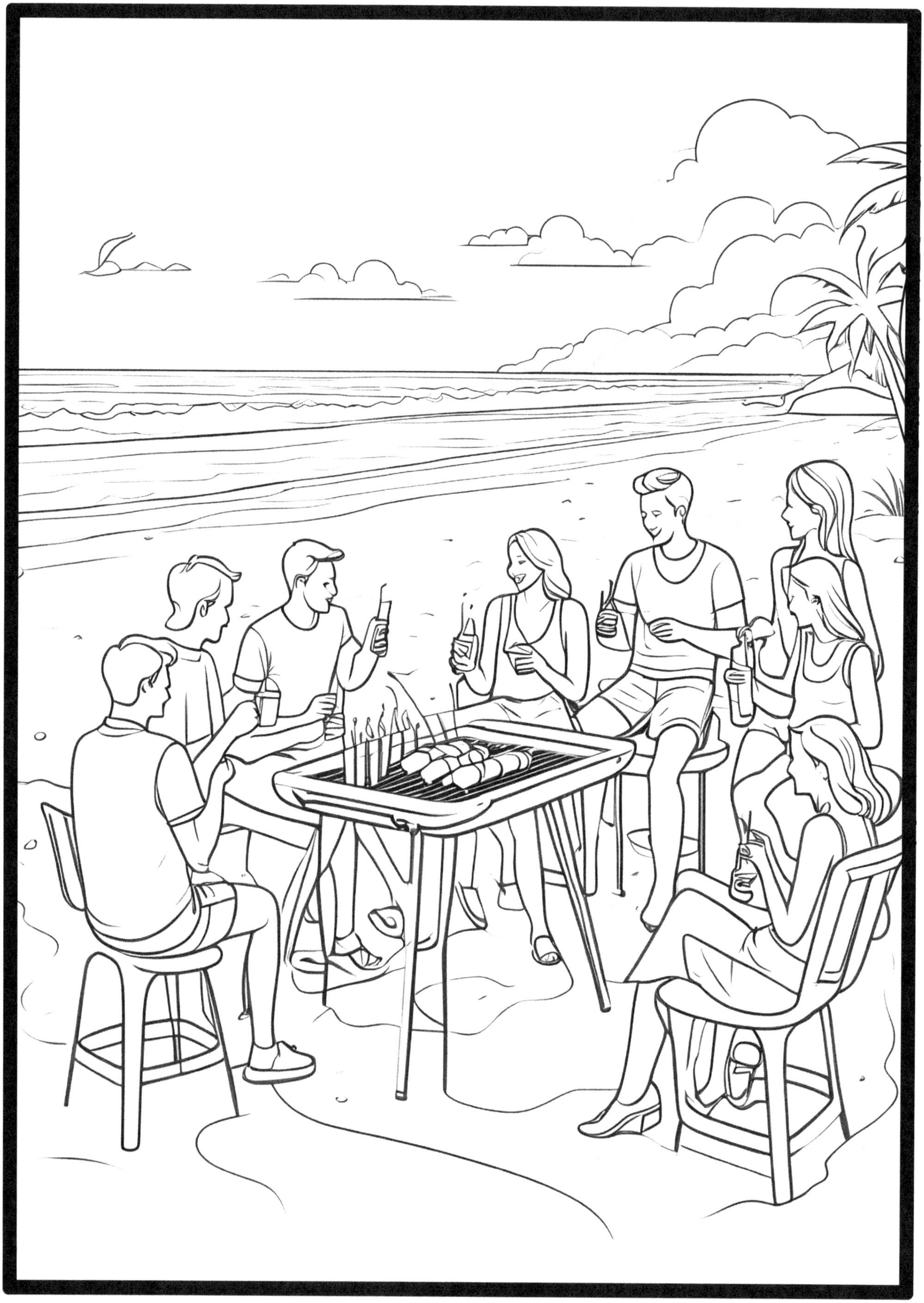

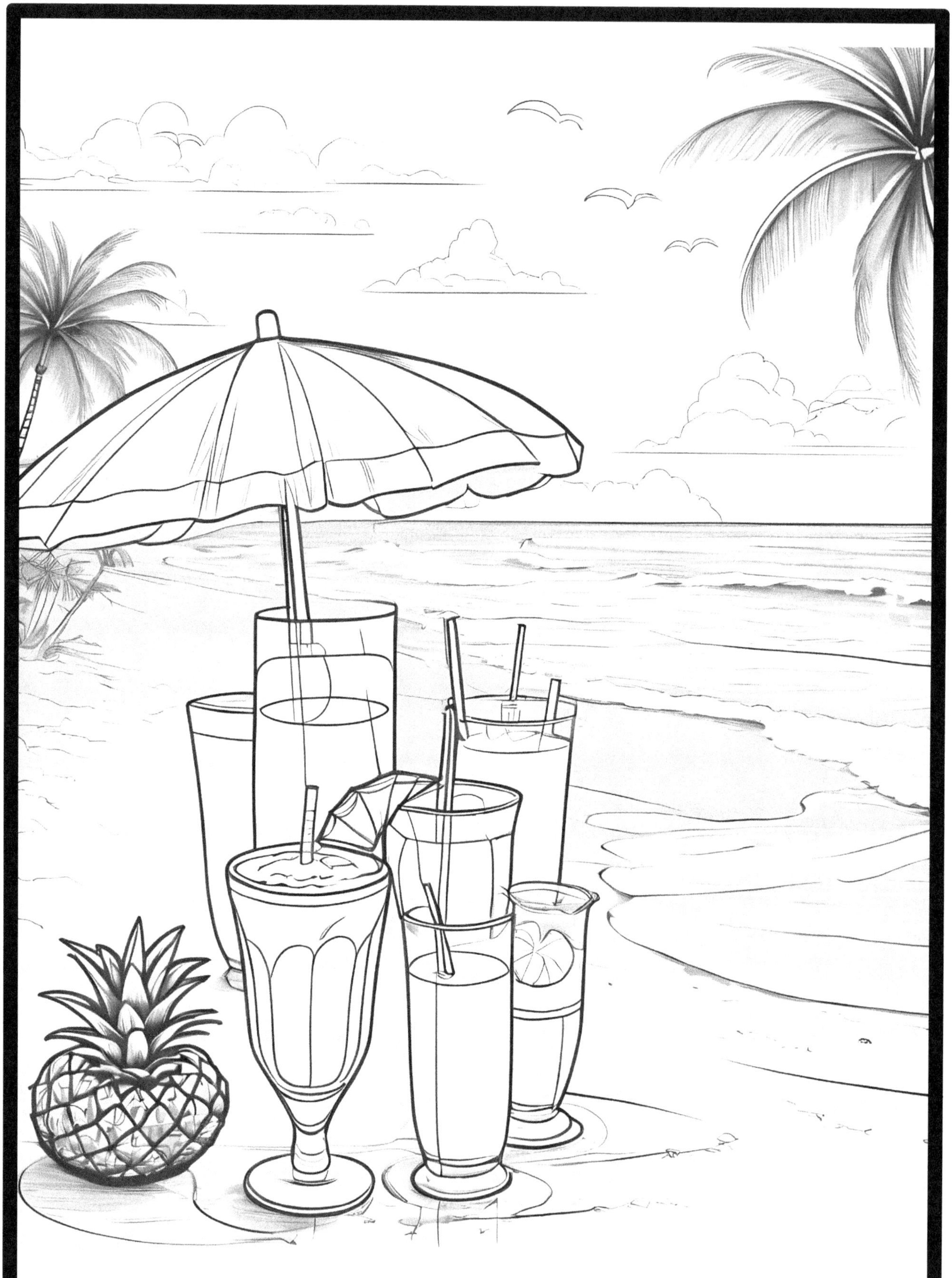

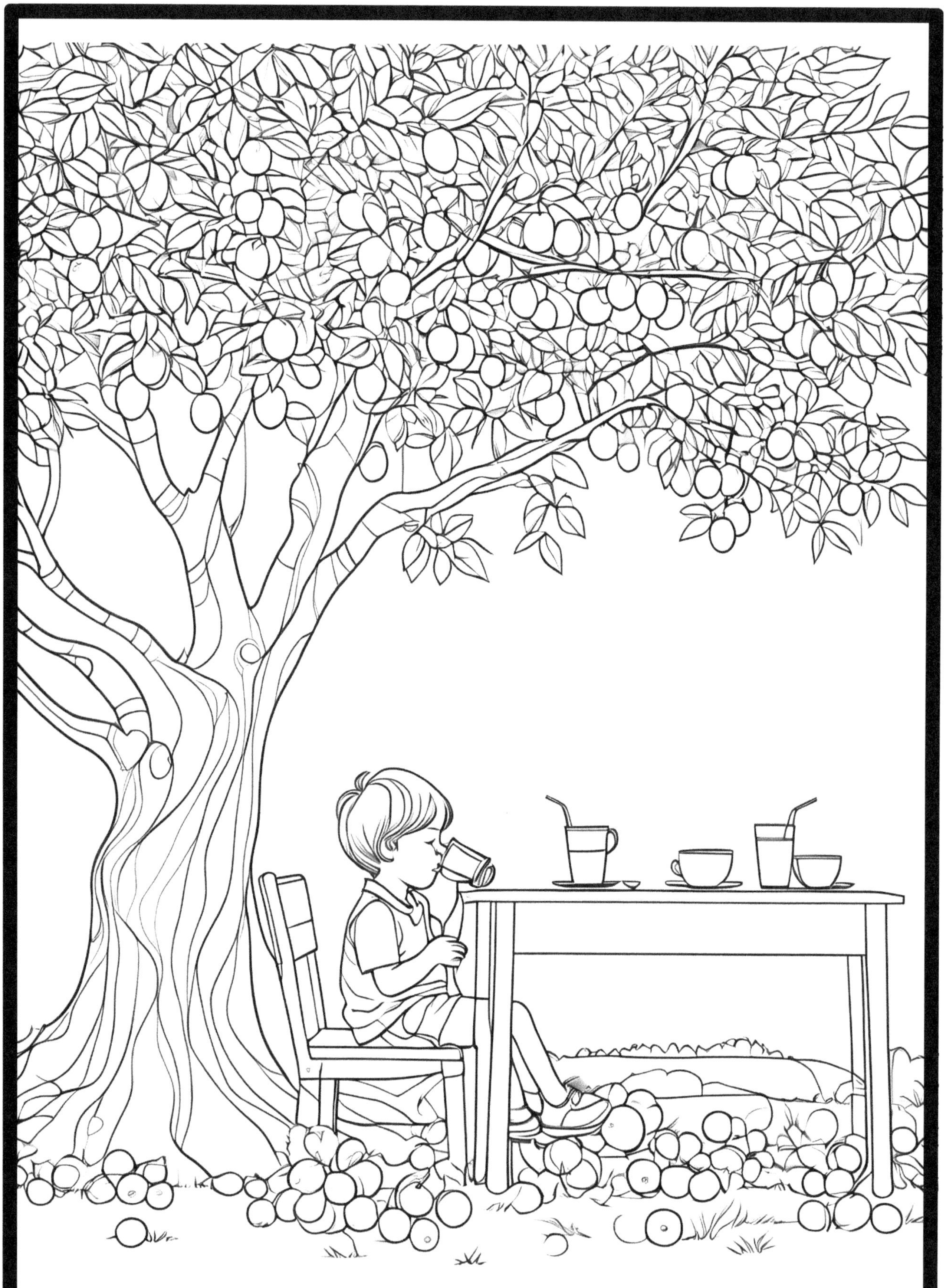

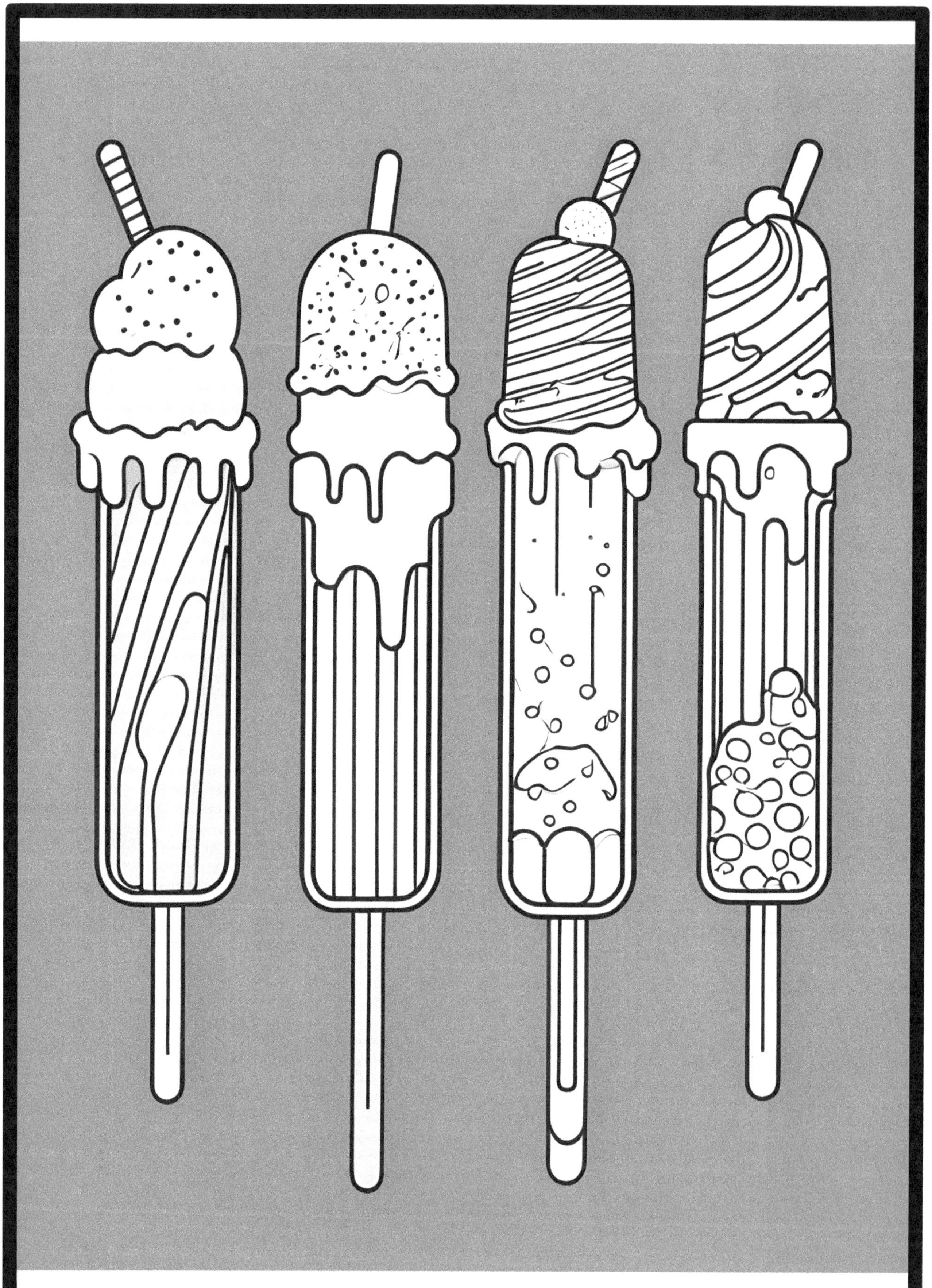

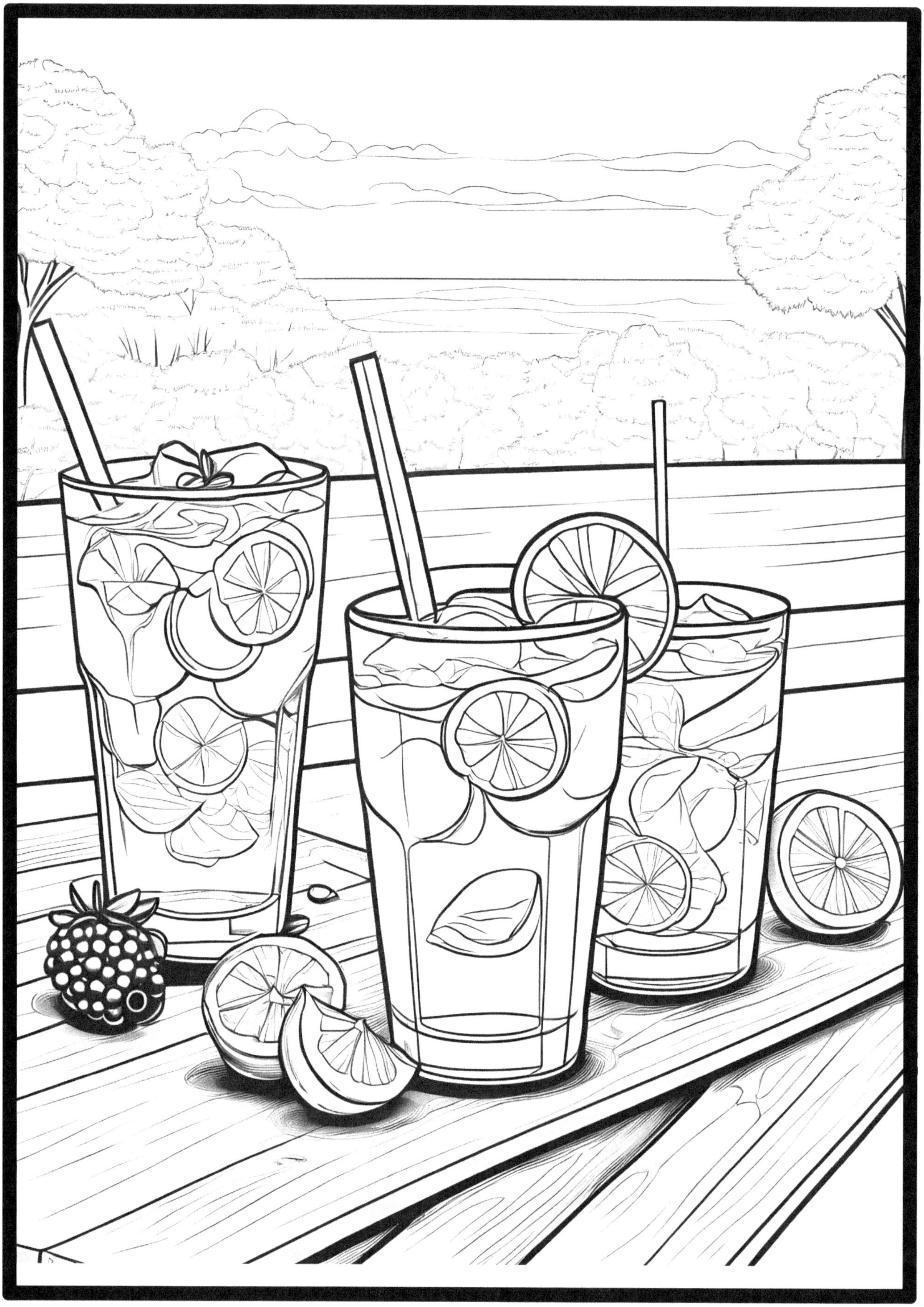

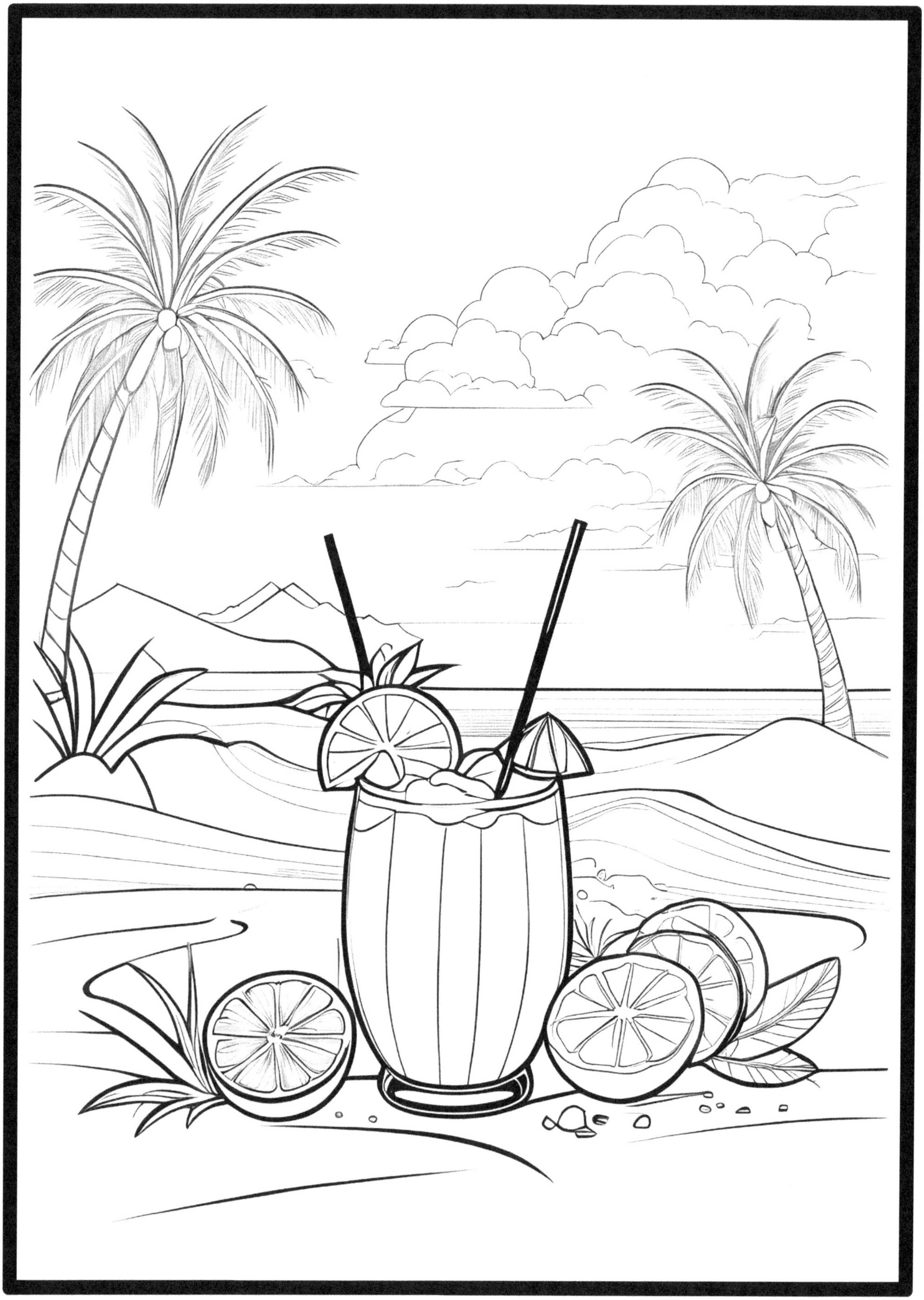

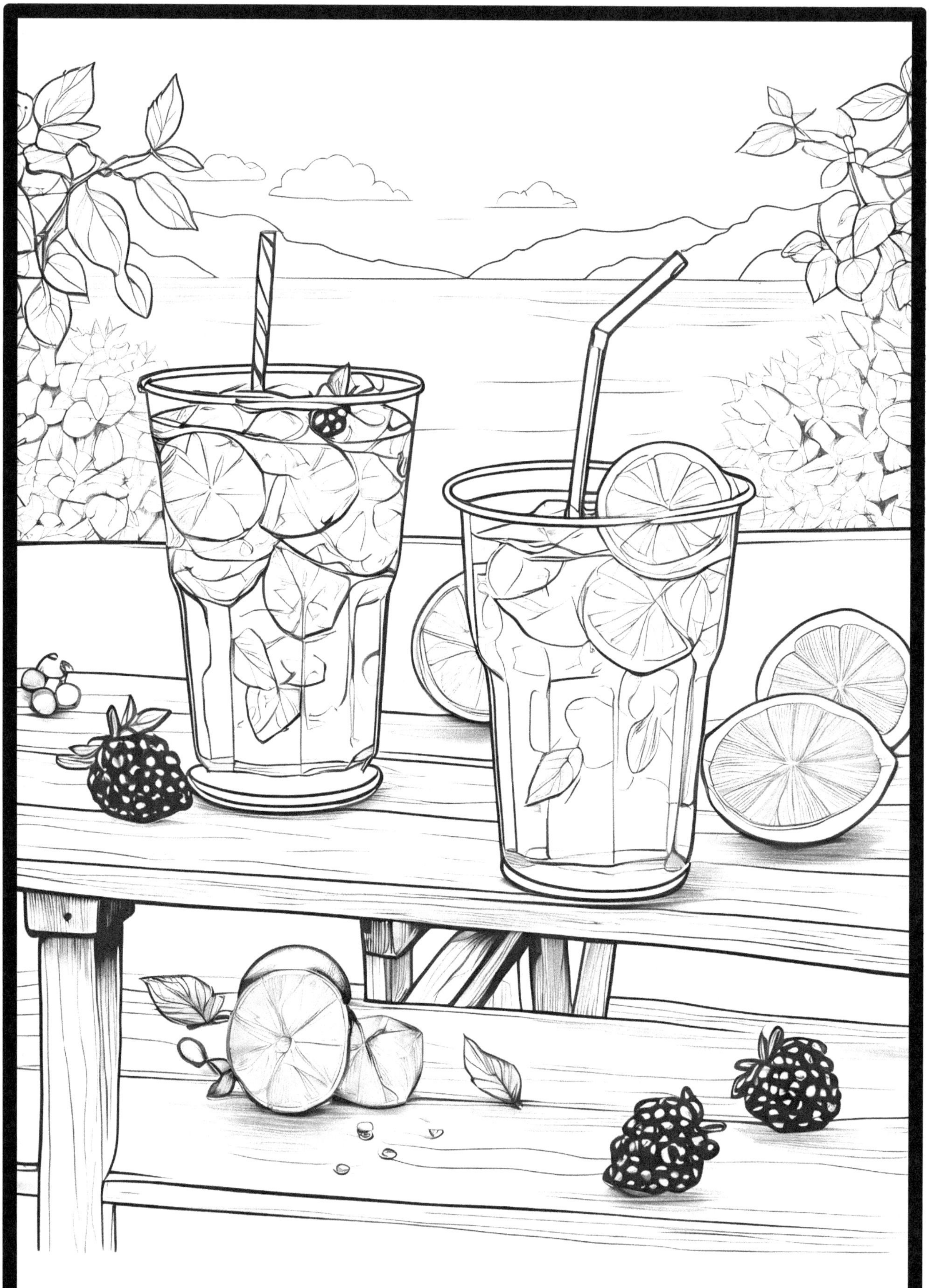

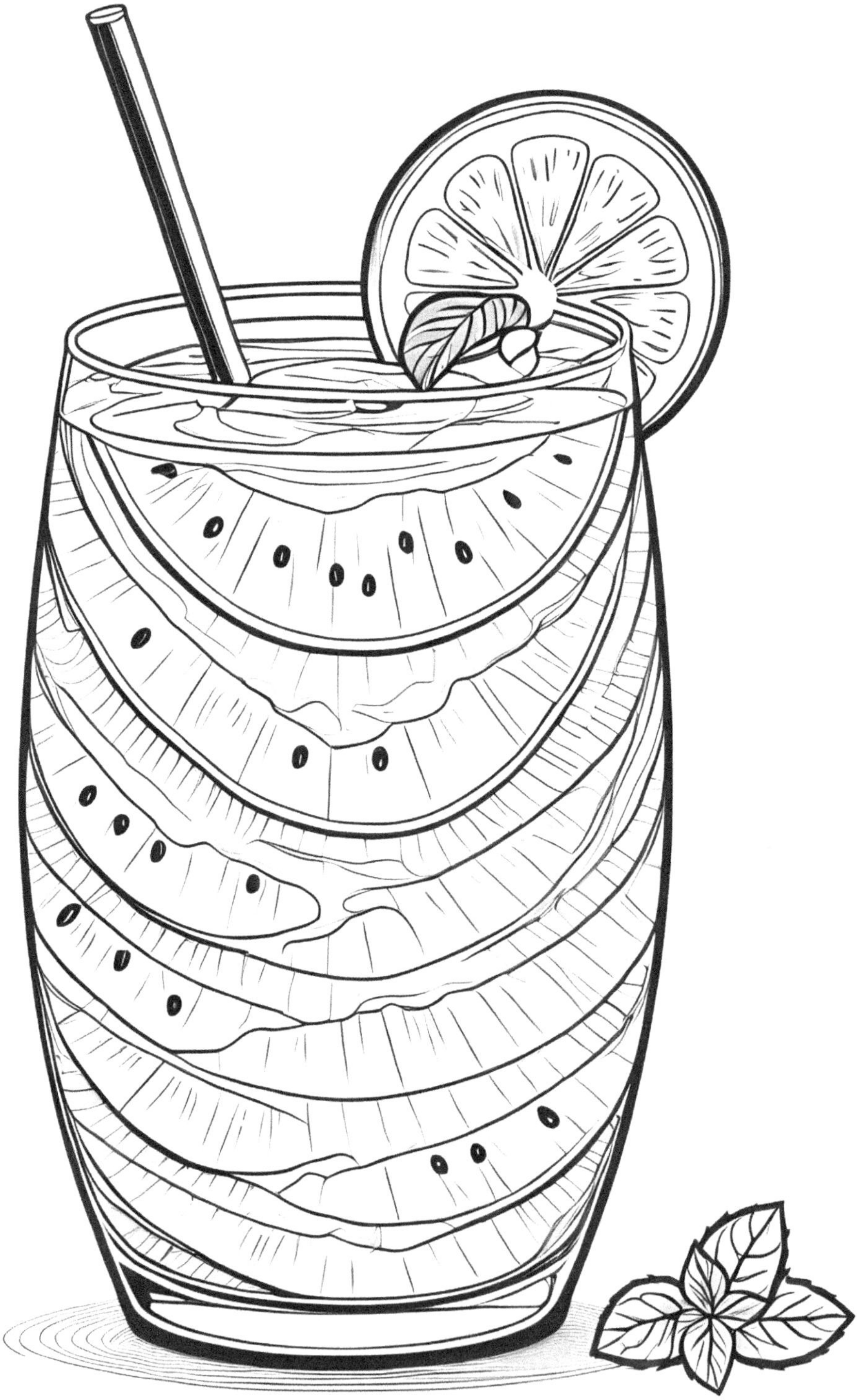

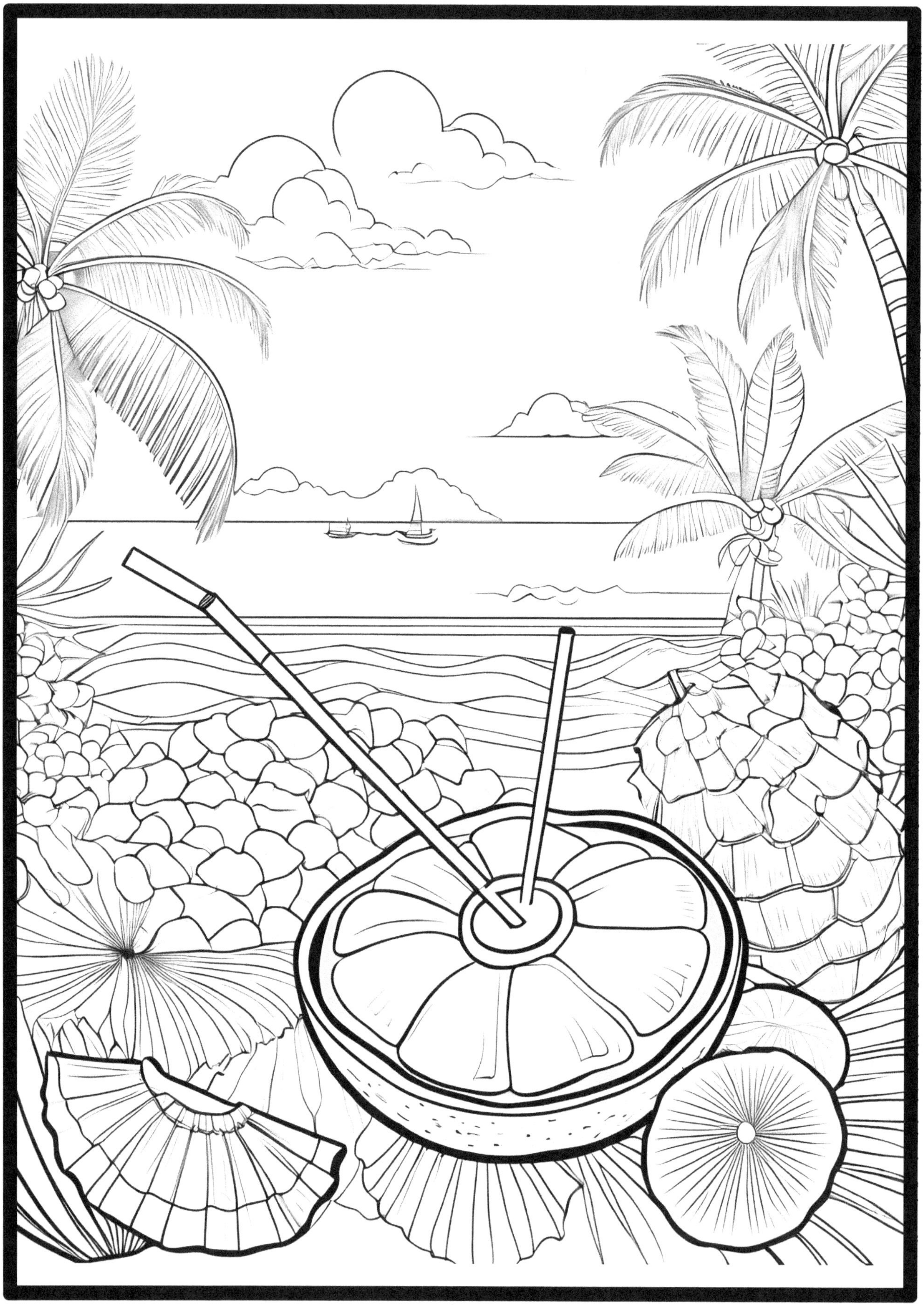

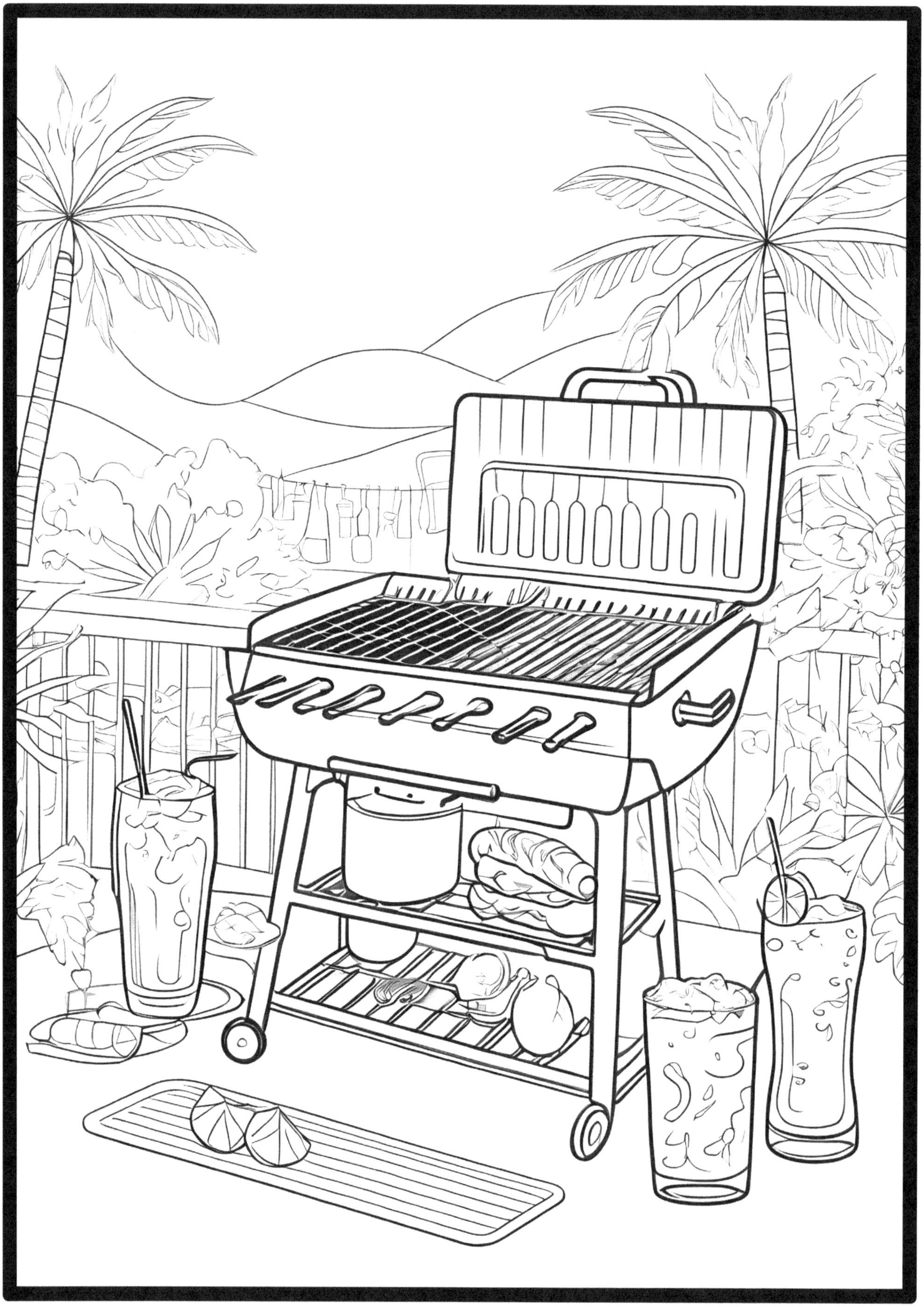

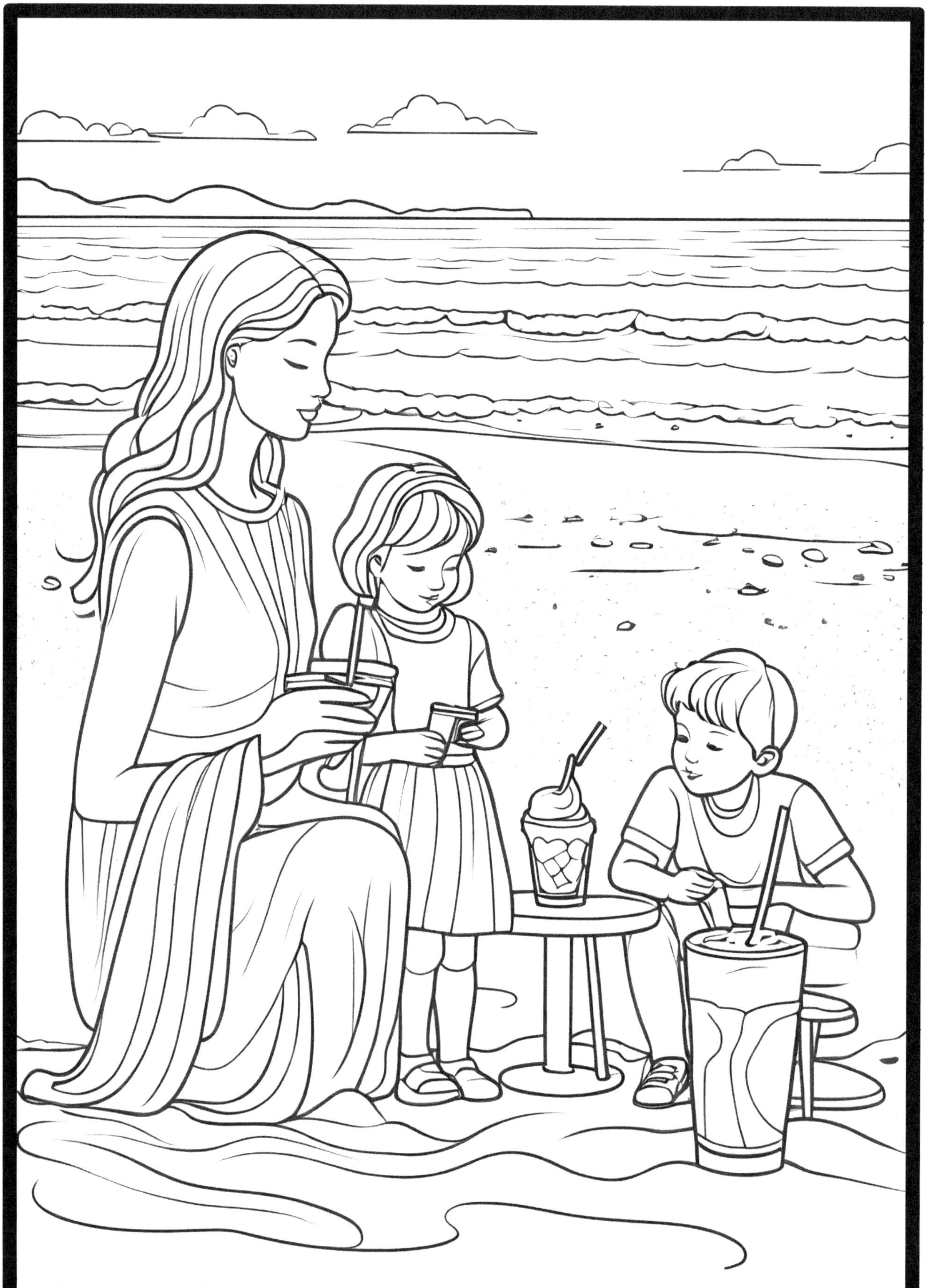

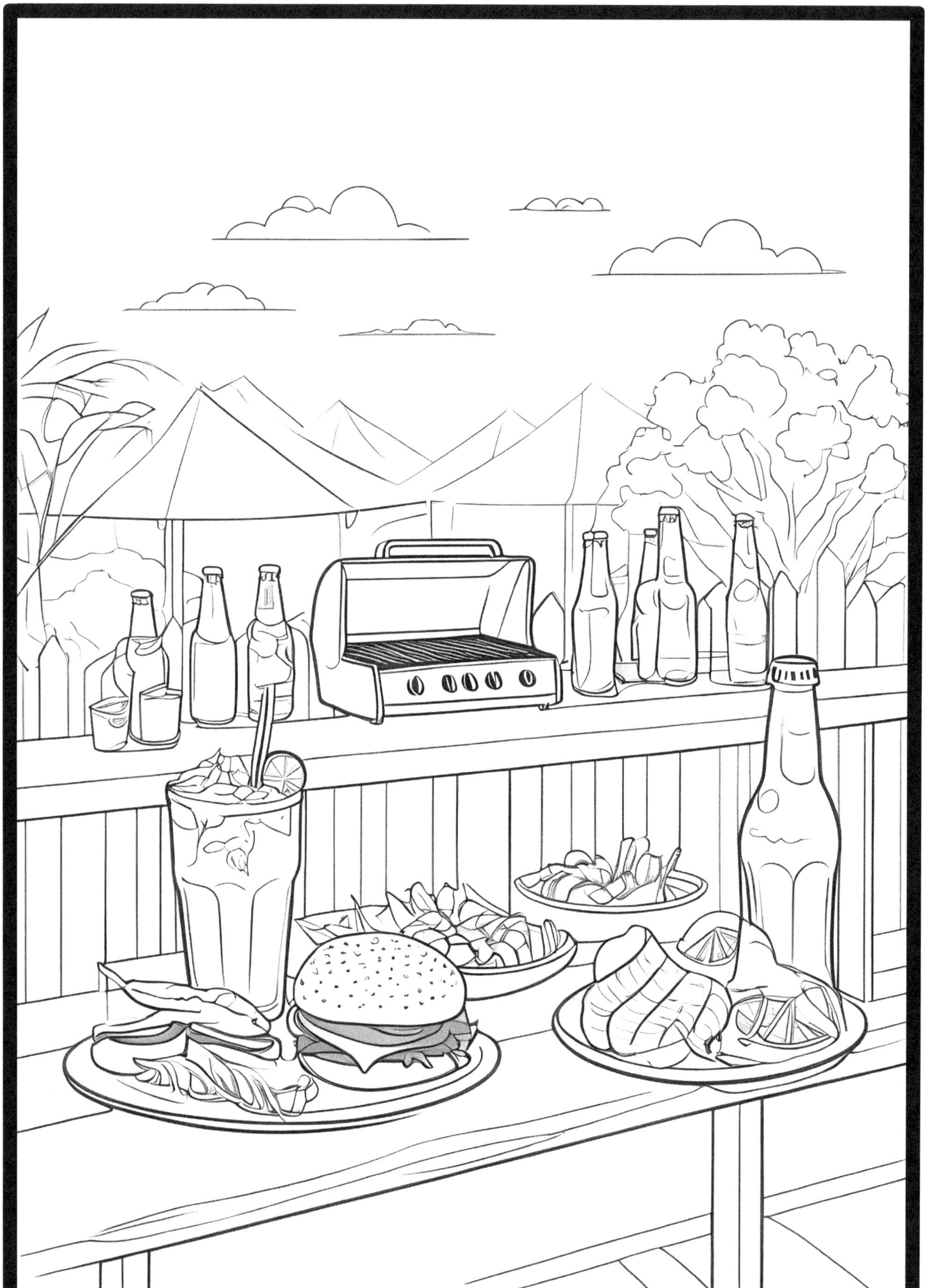

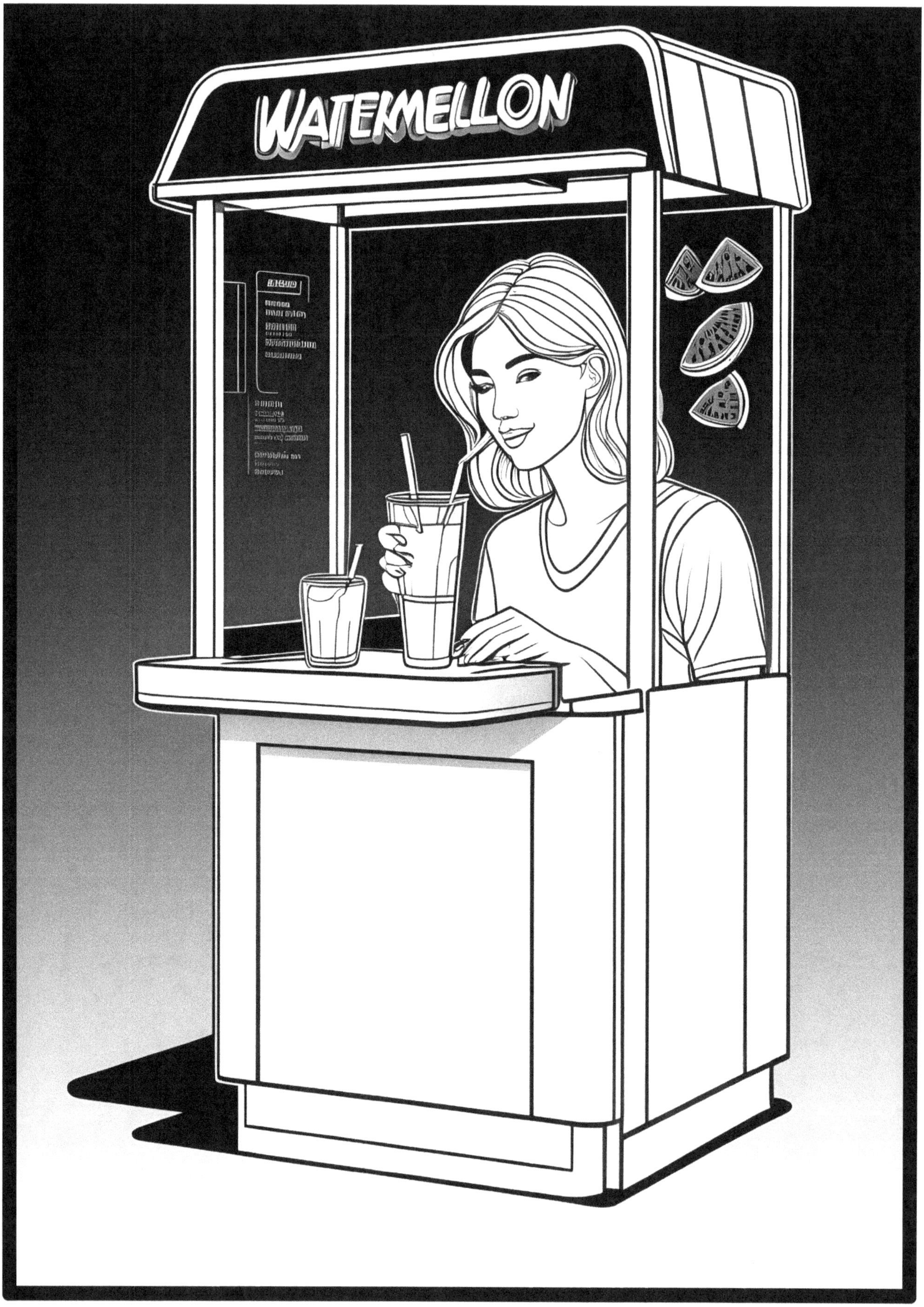
WATERMELLON

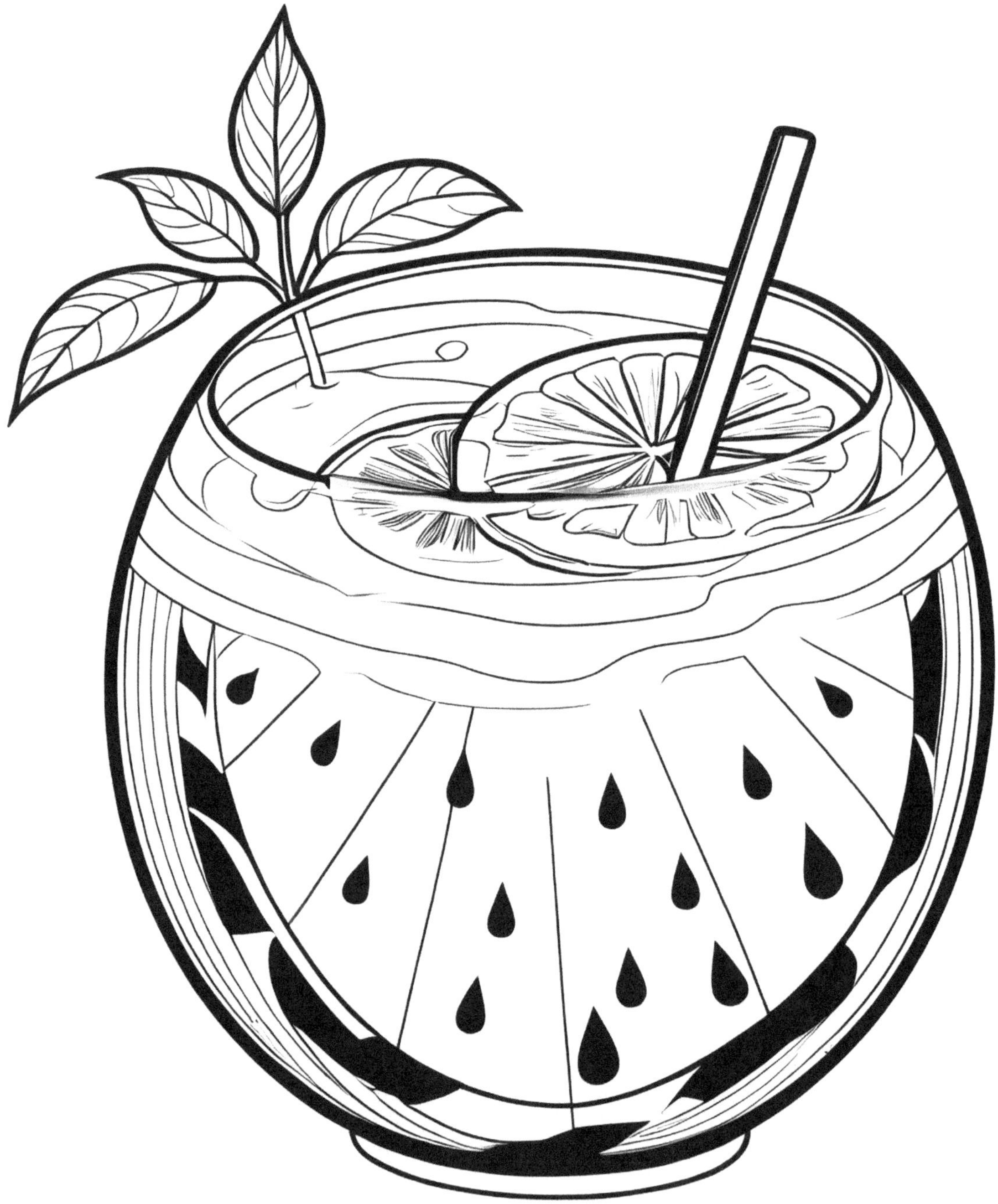

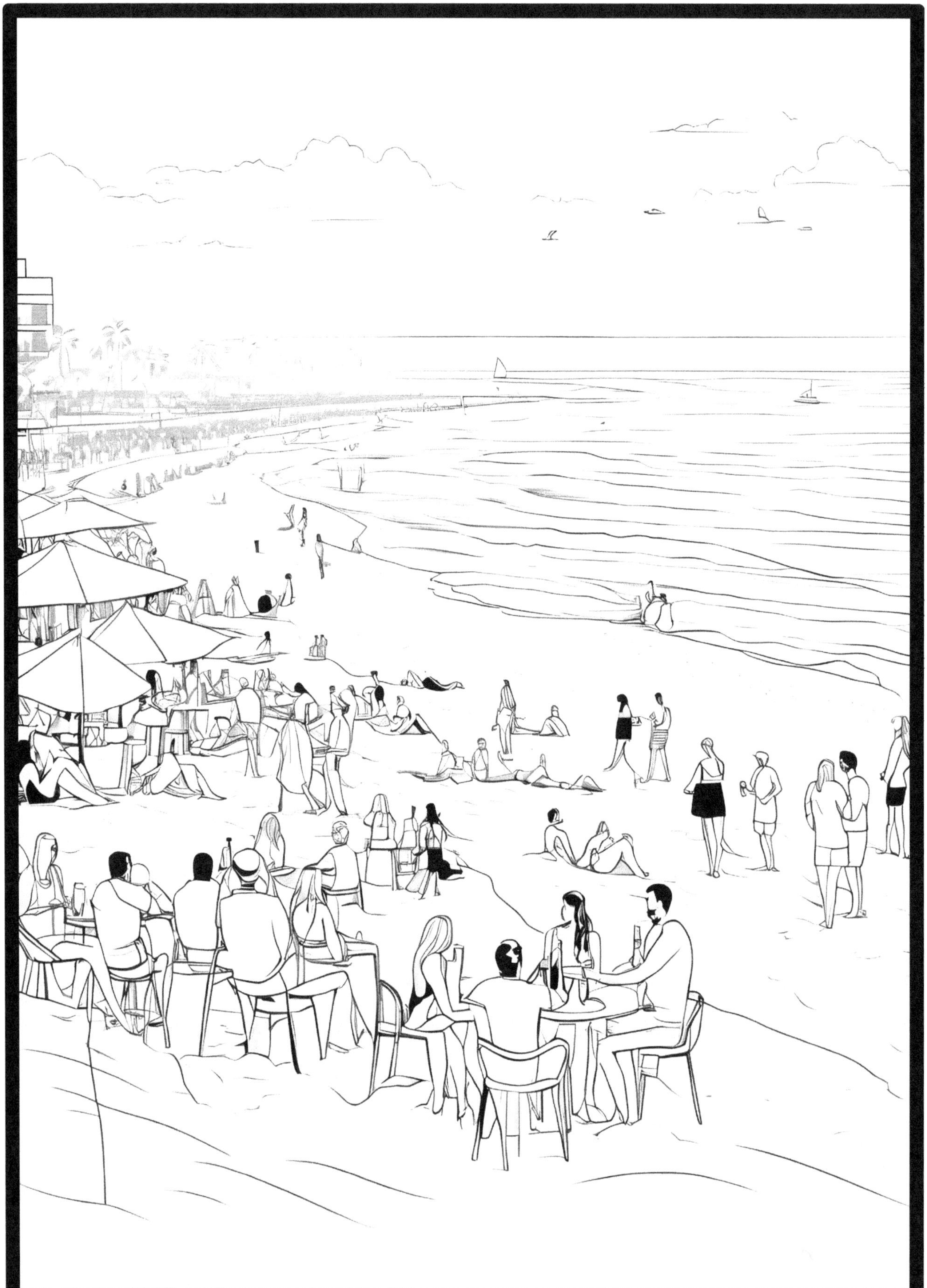

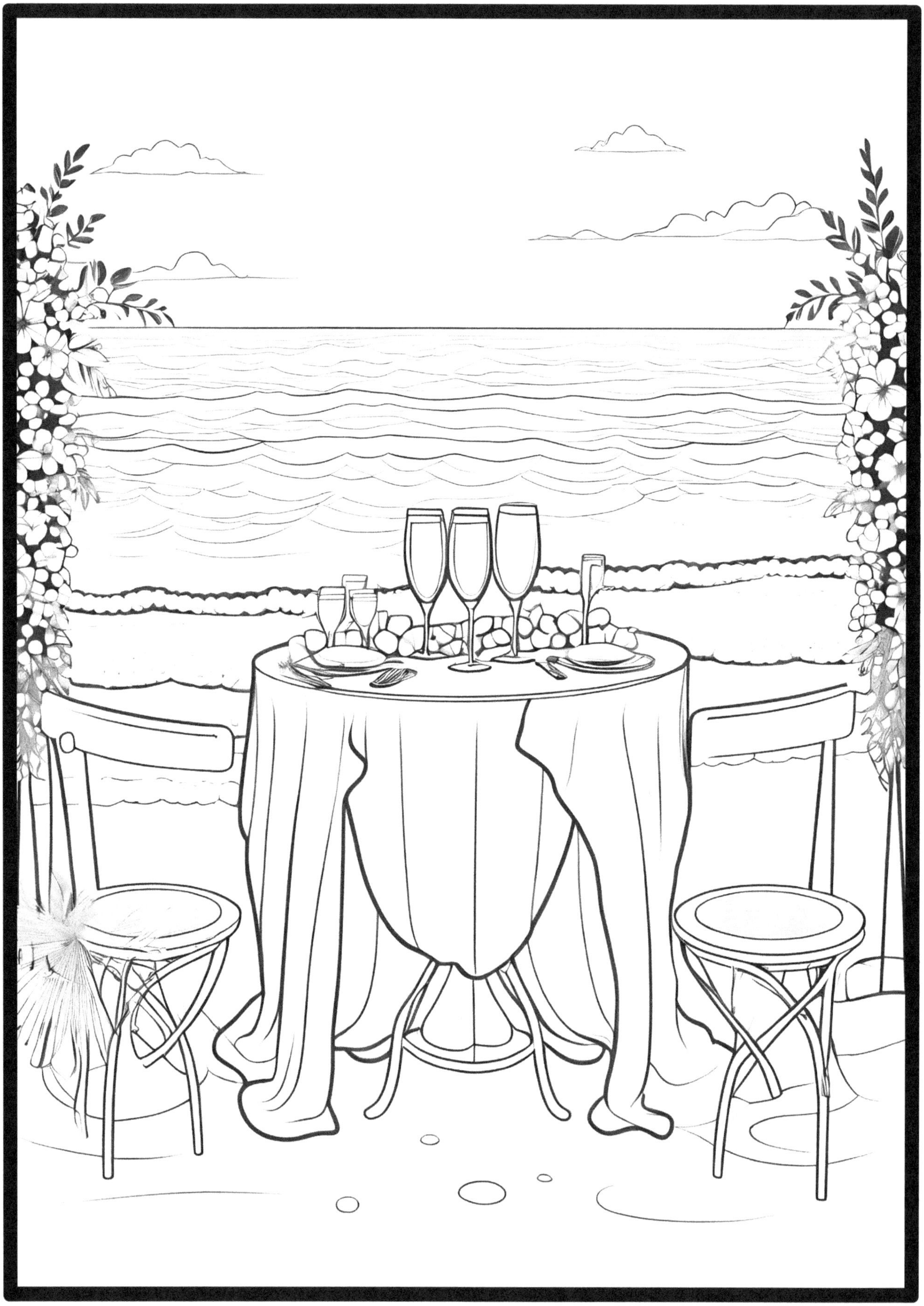

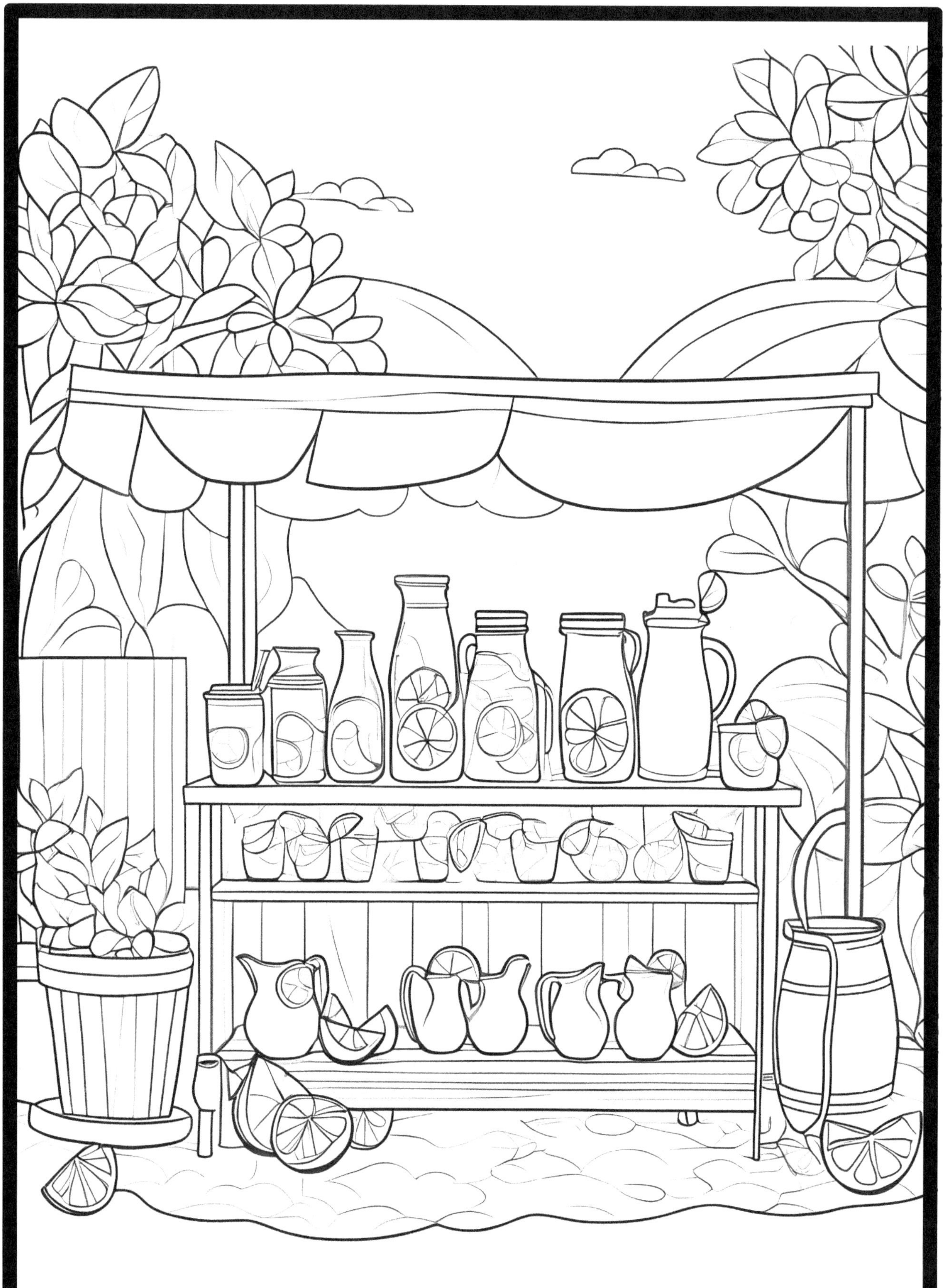

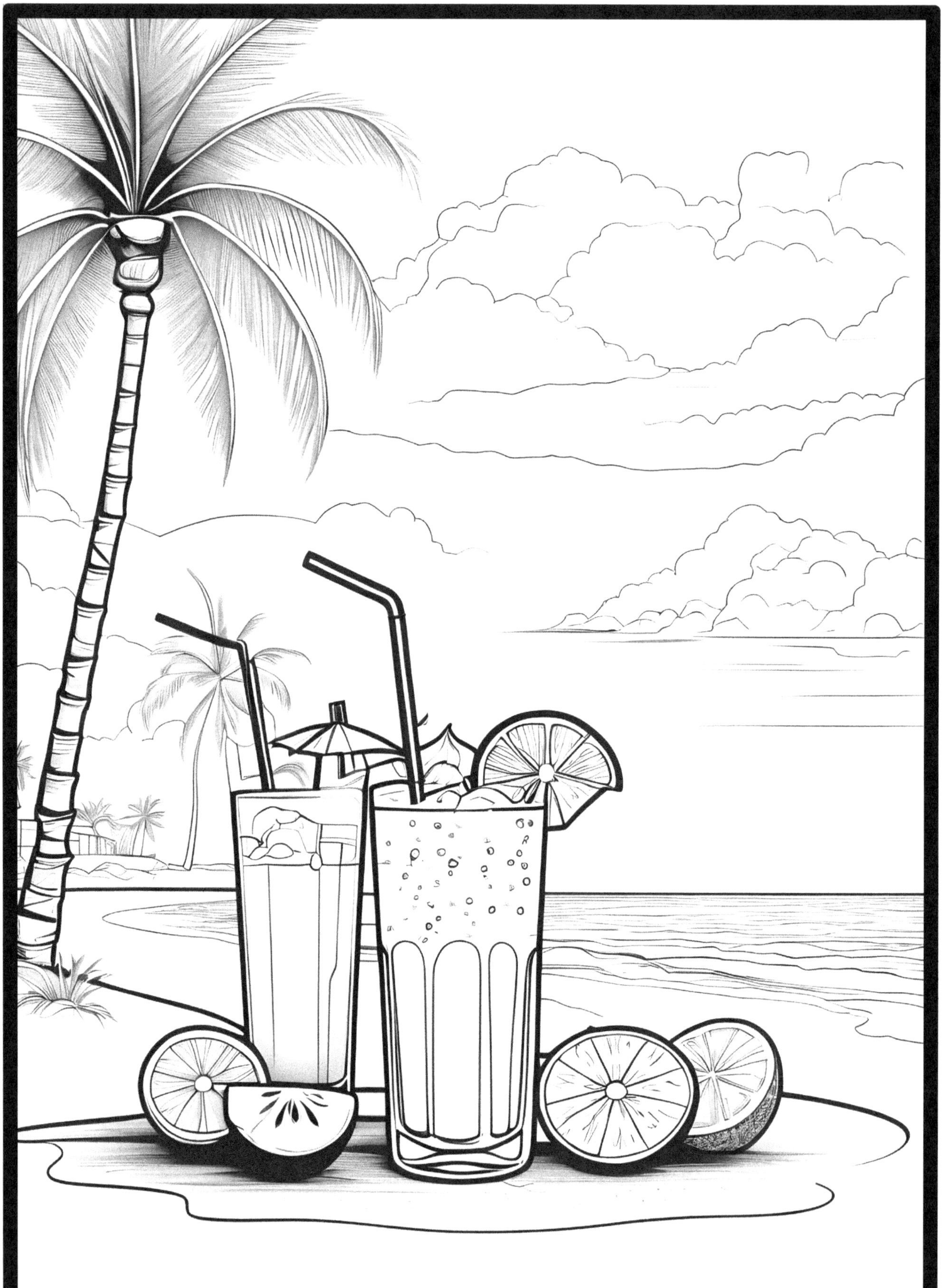

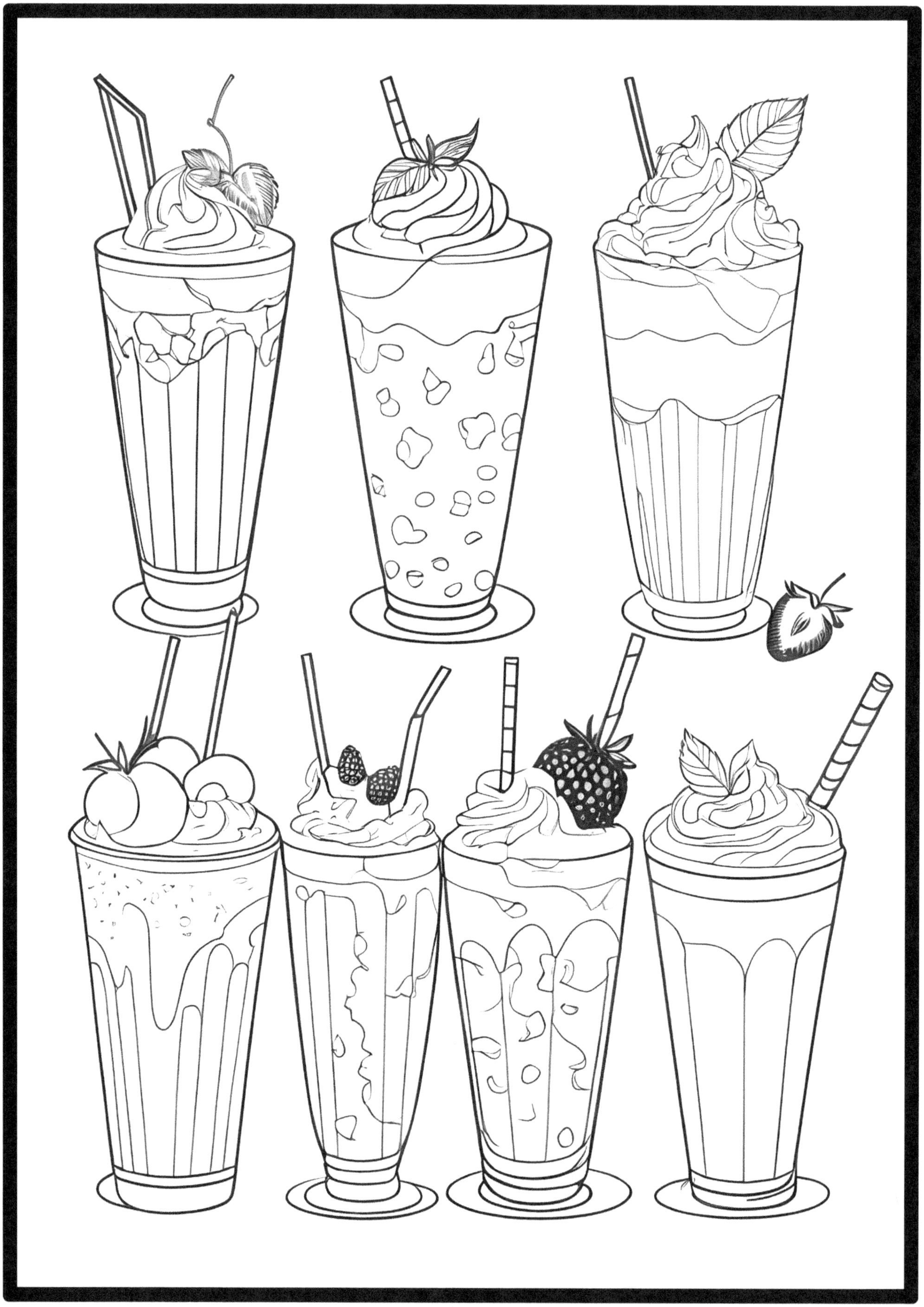

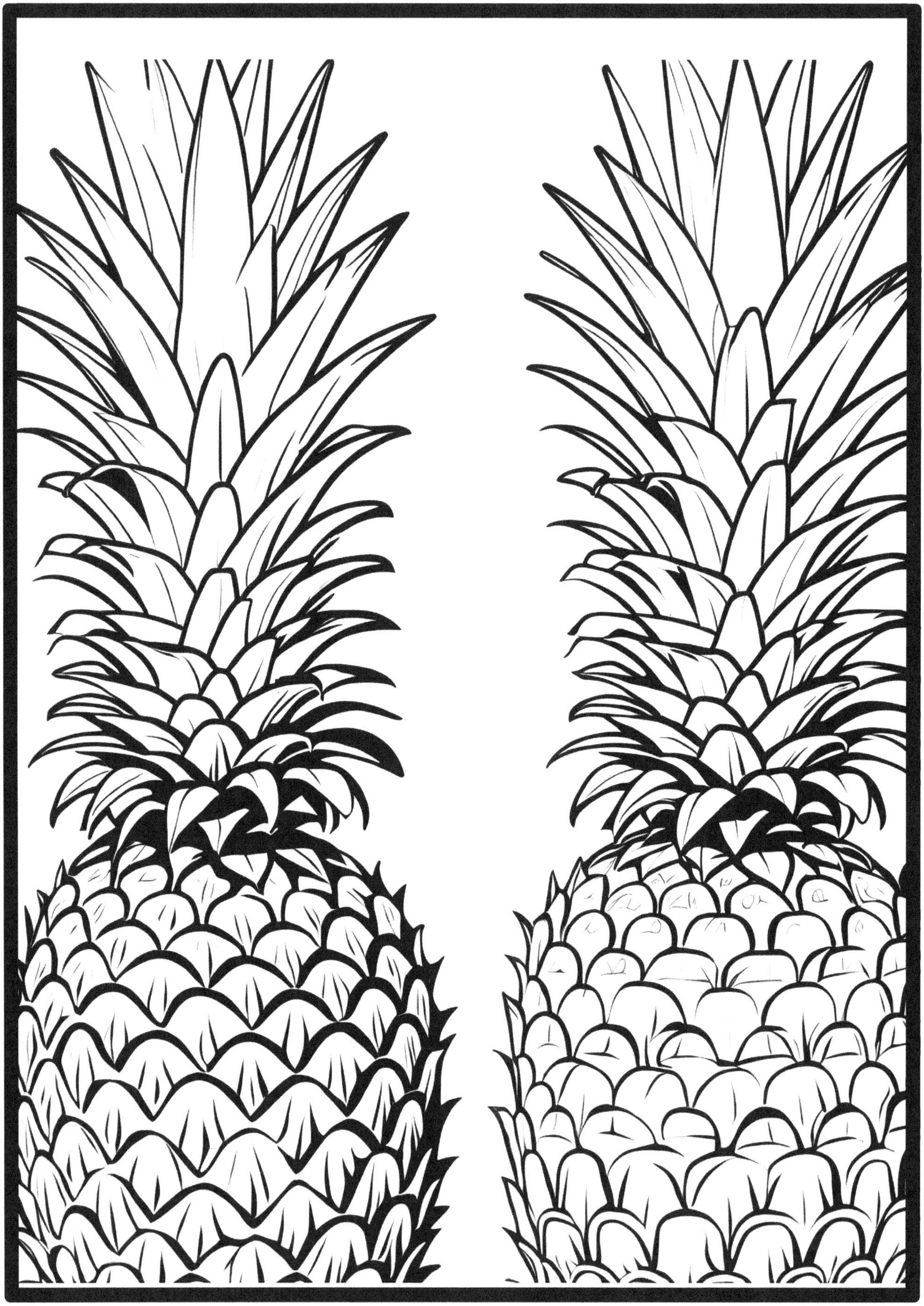

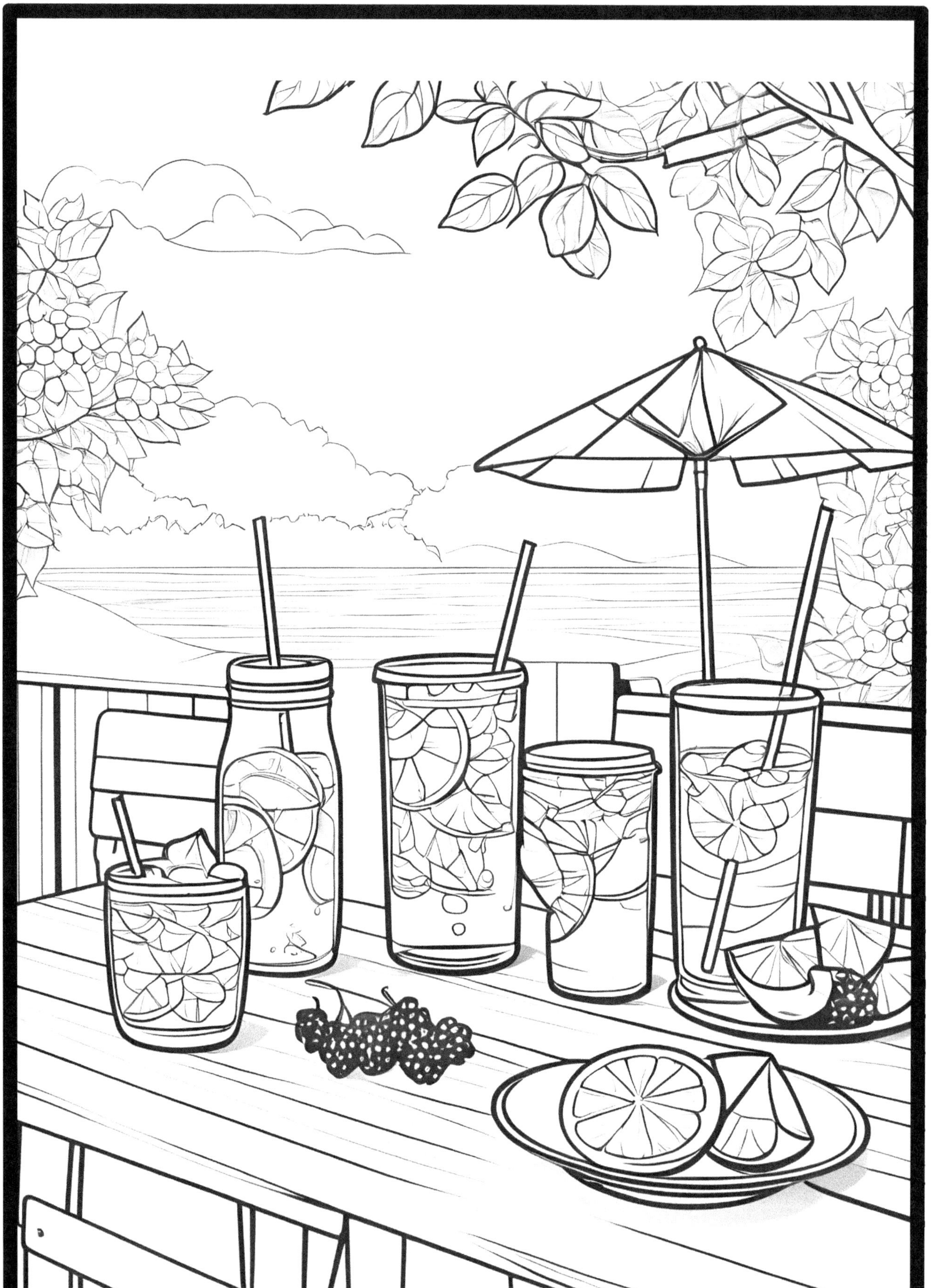

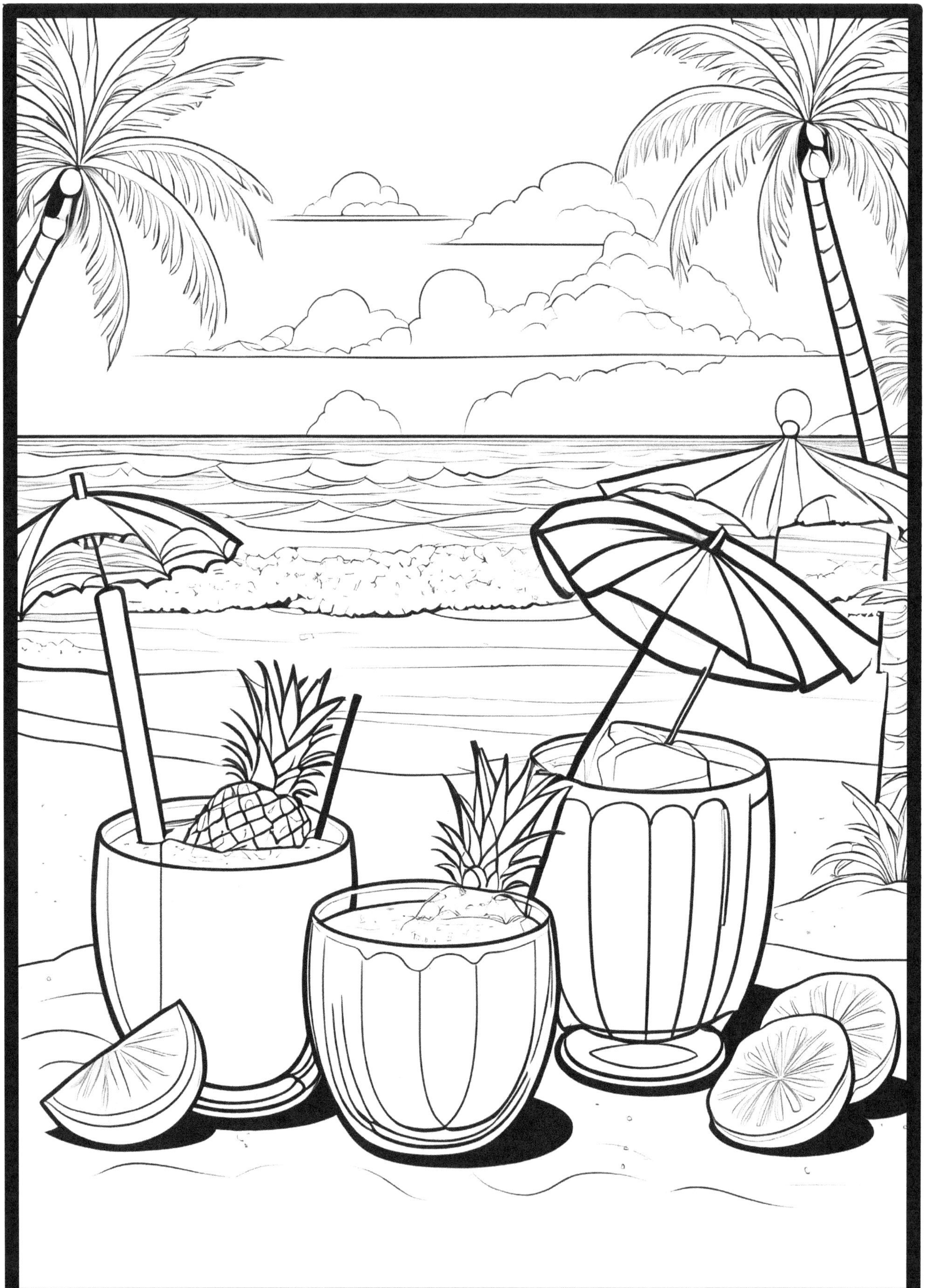

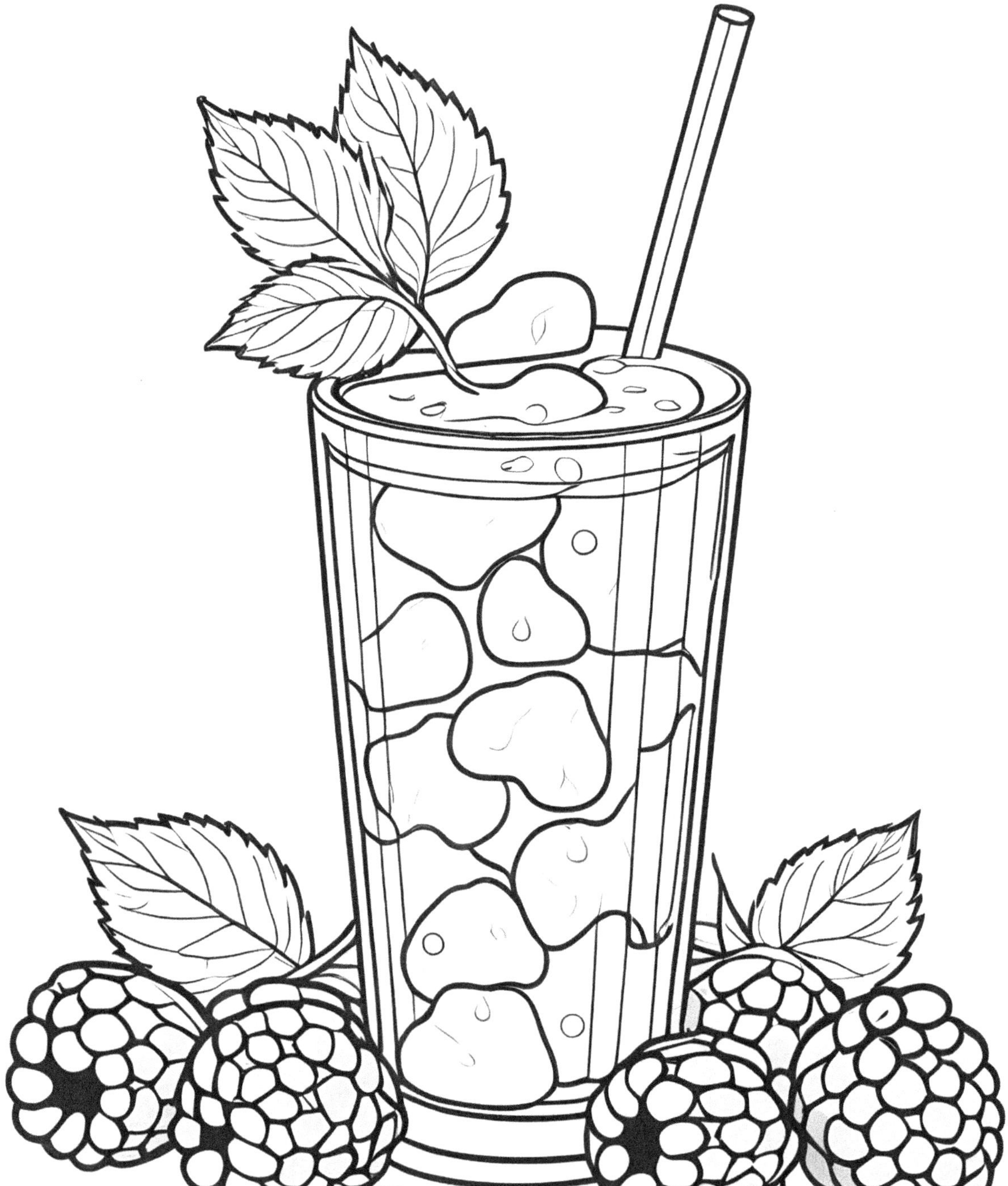

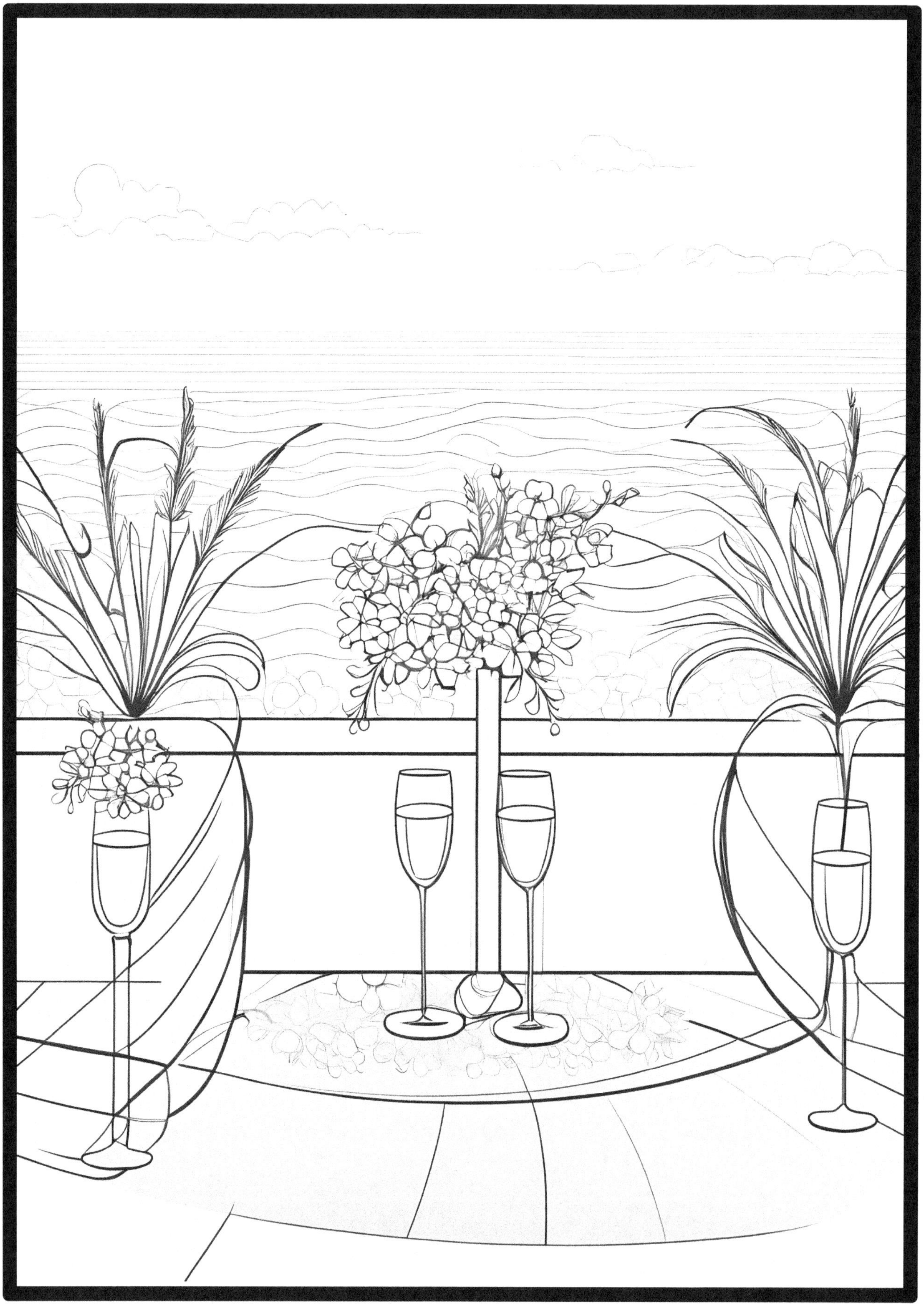

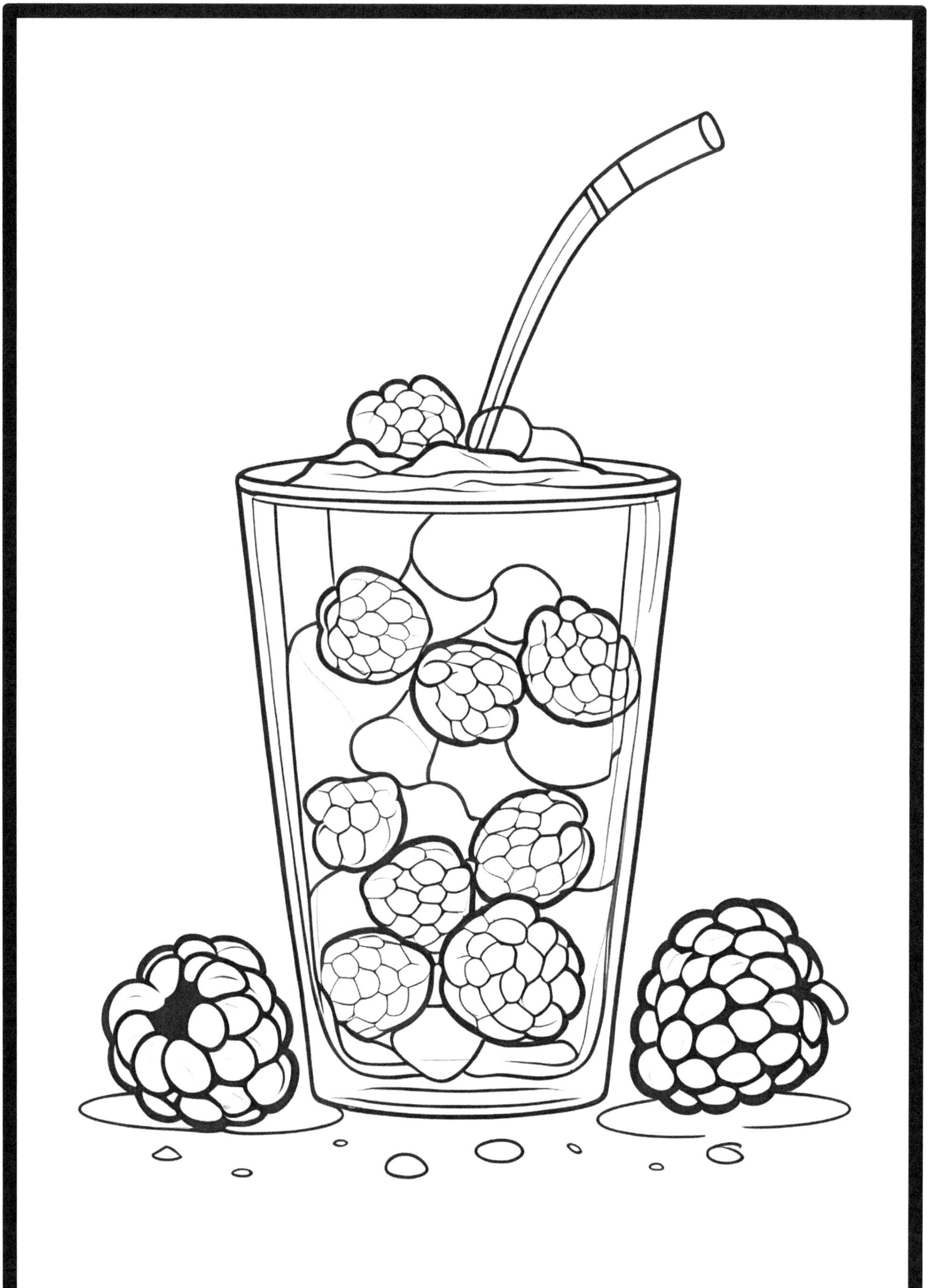

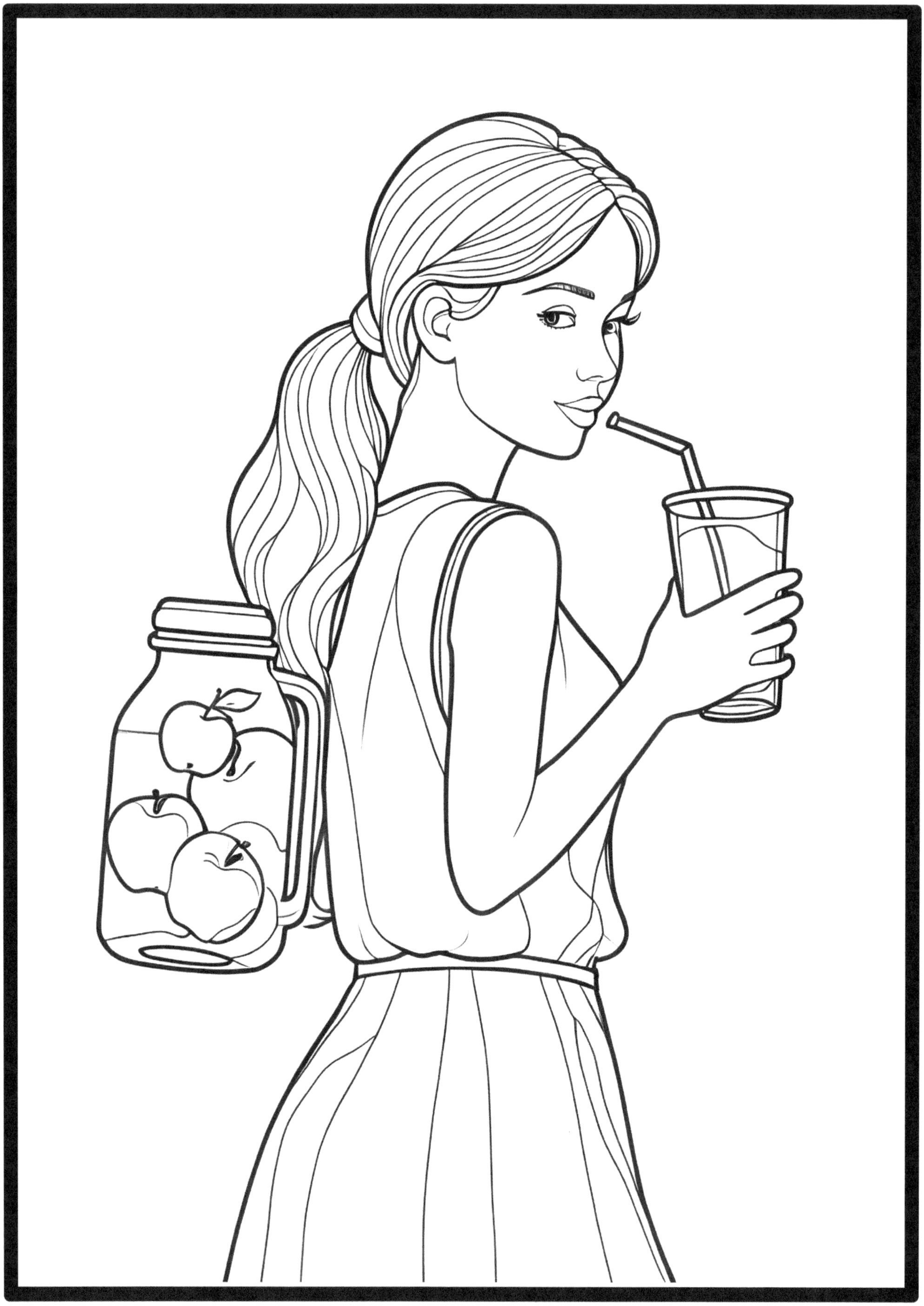

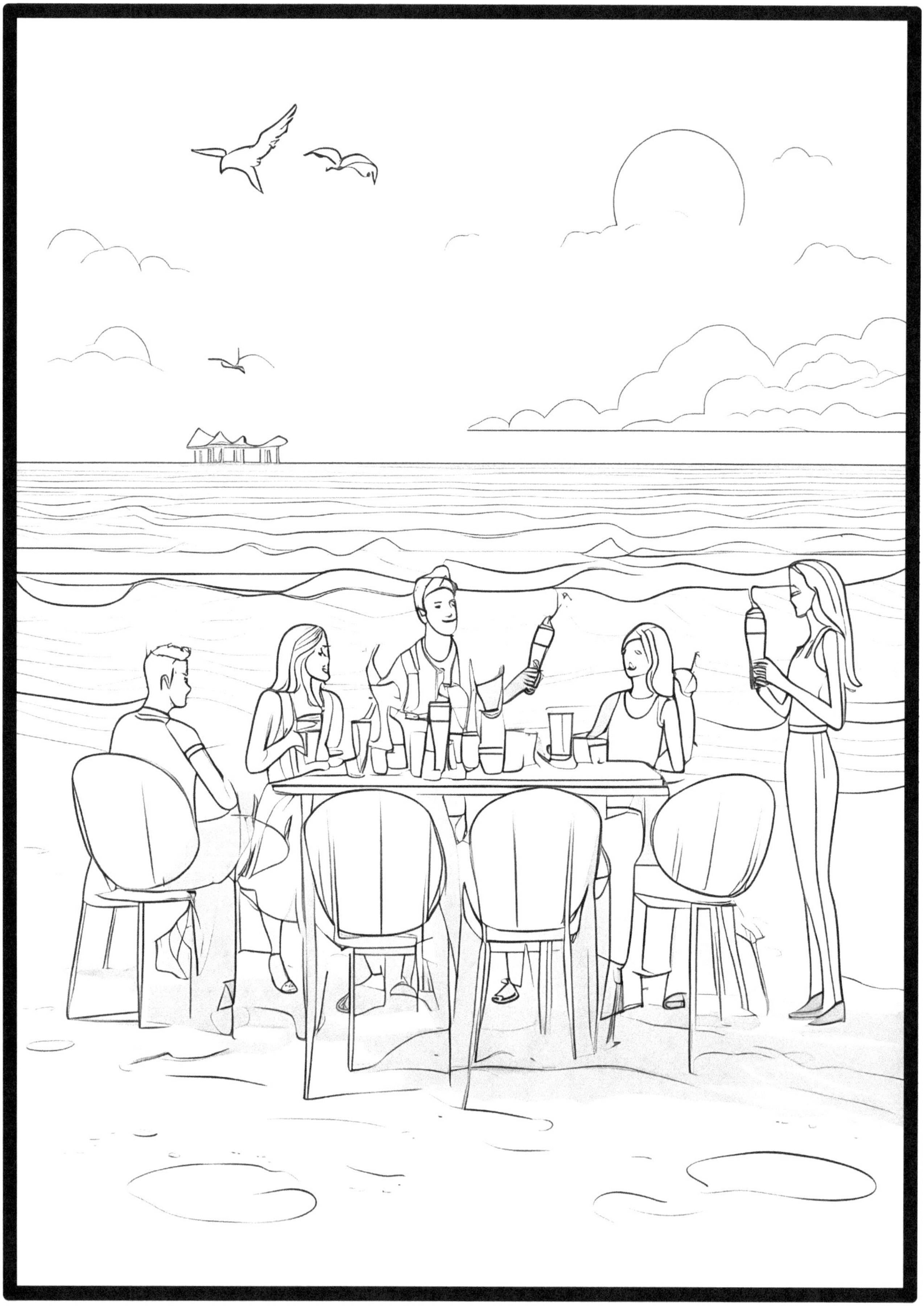

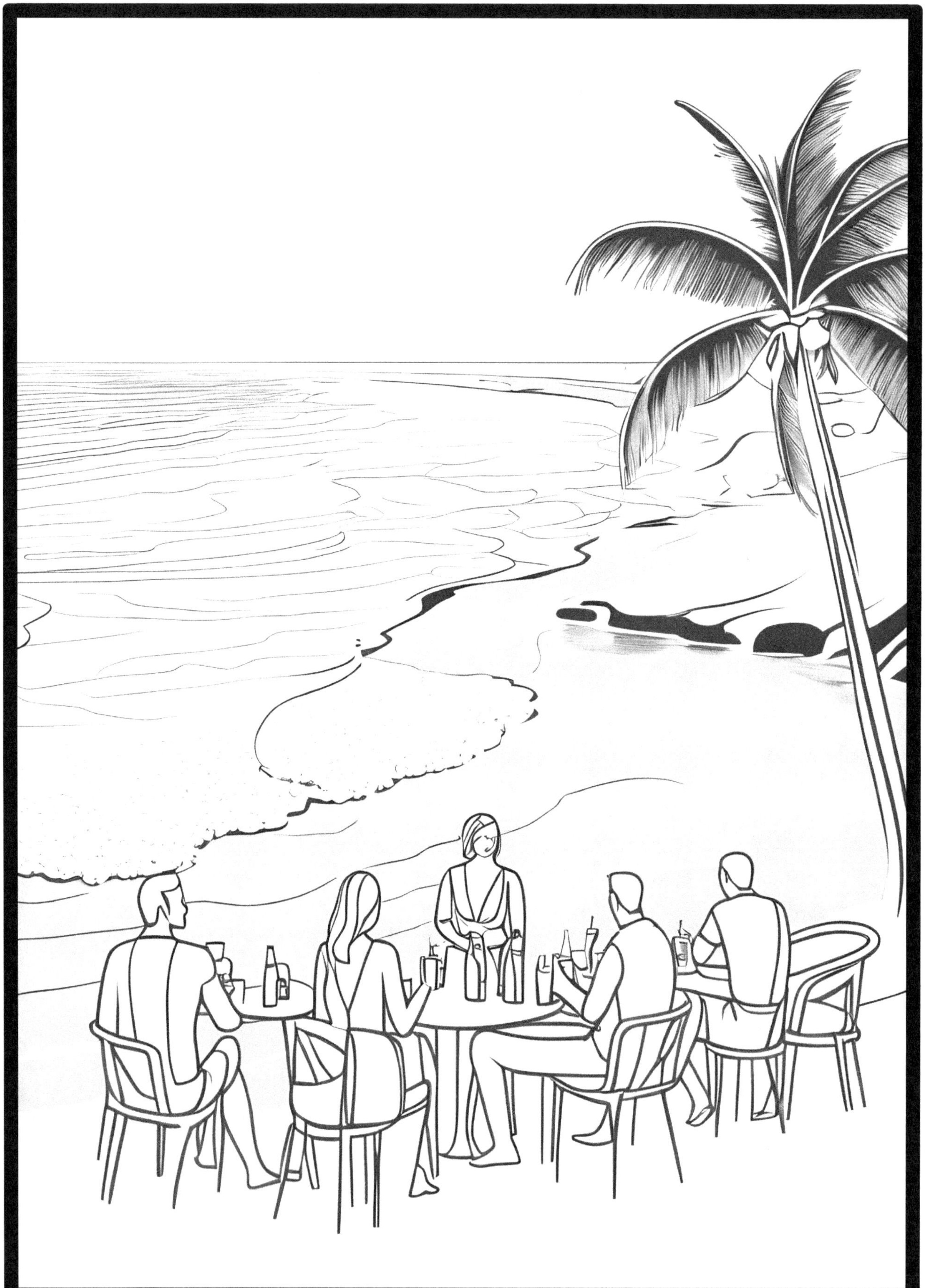

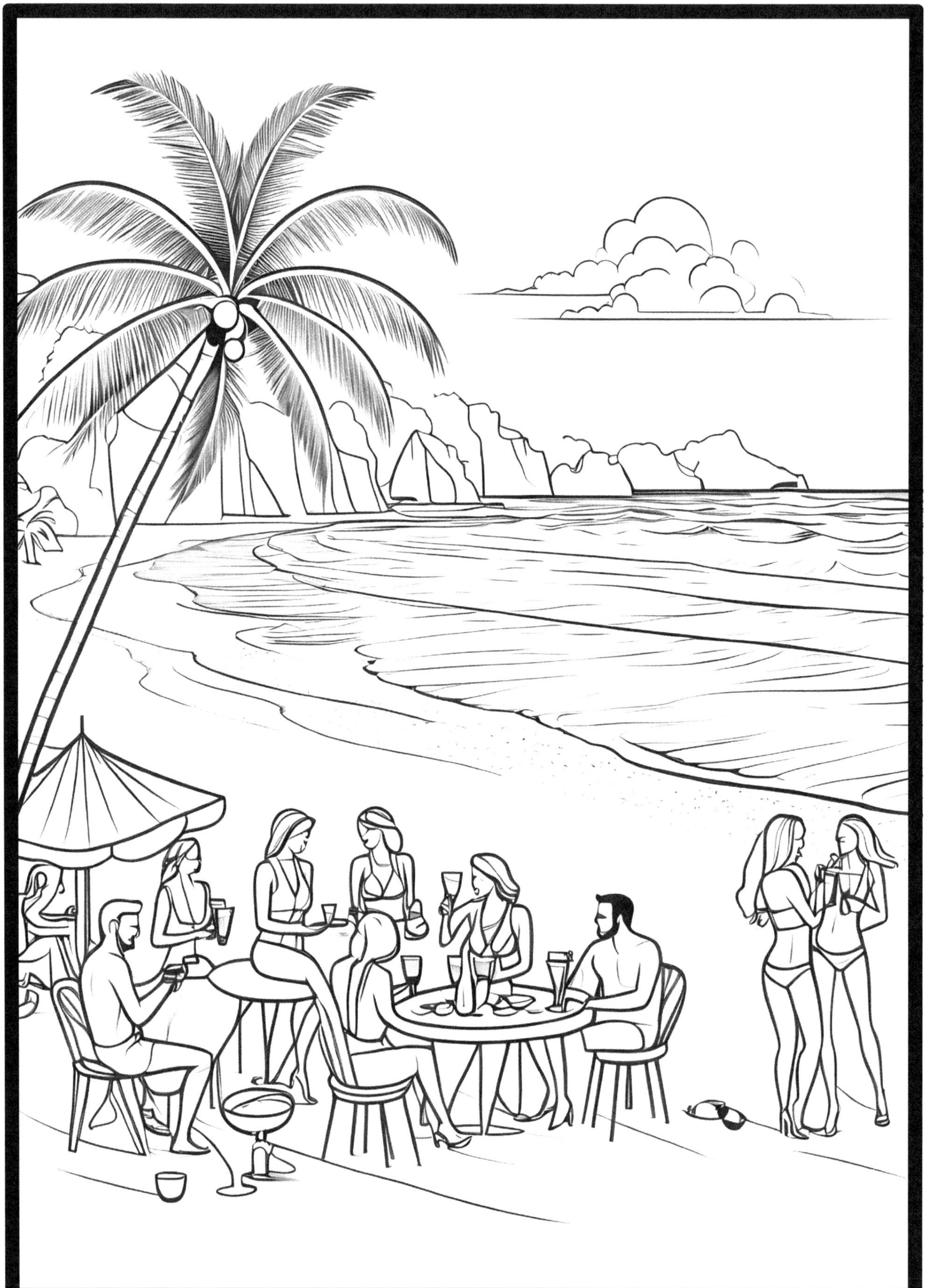

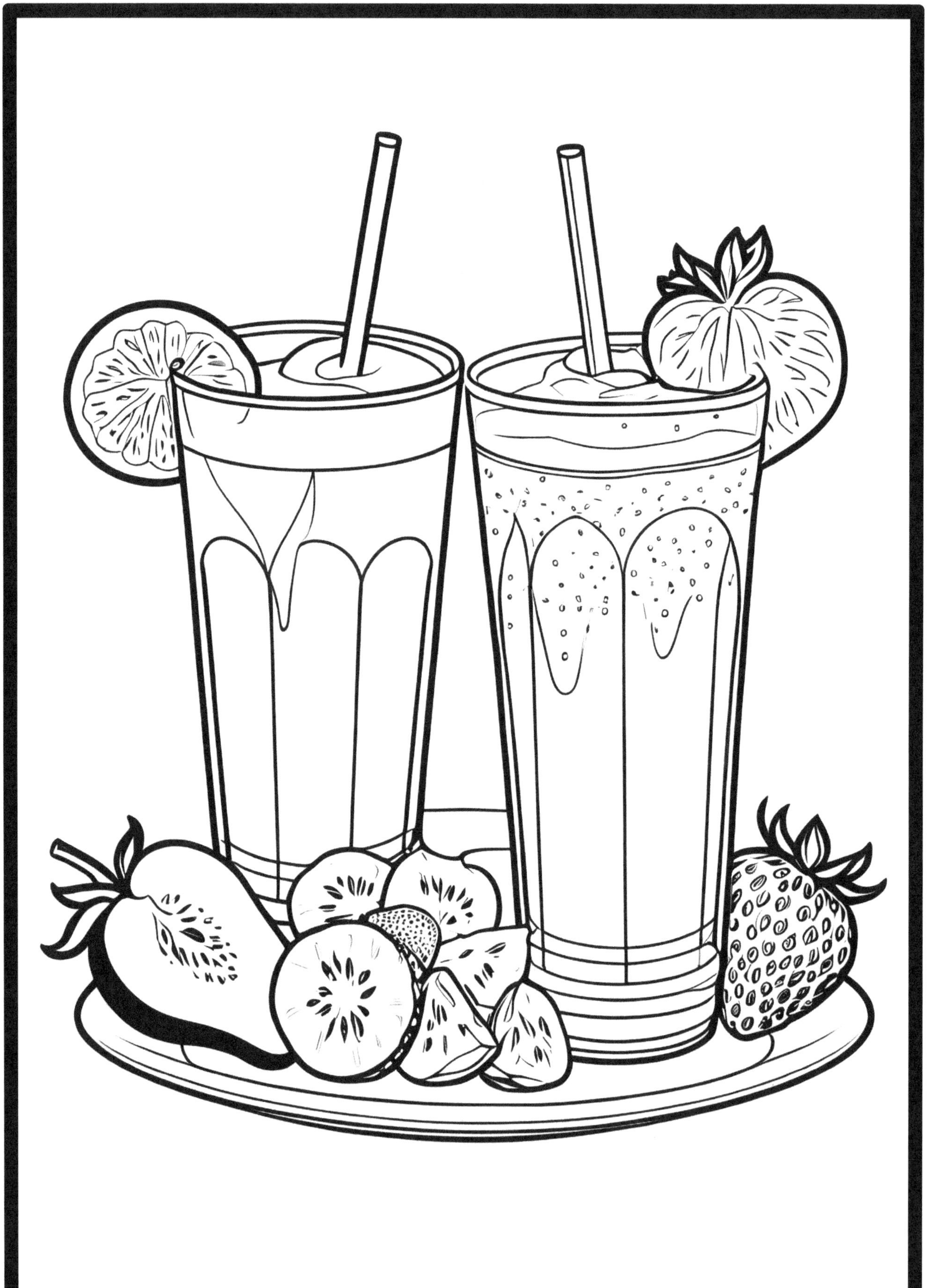

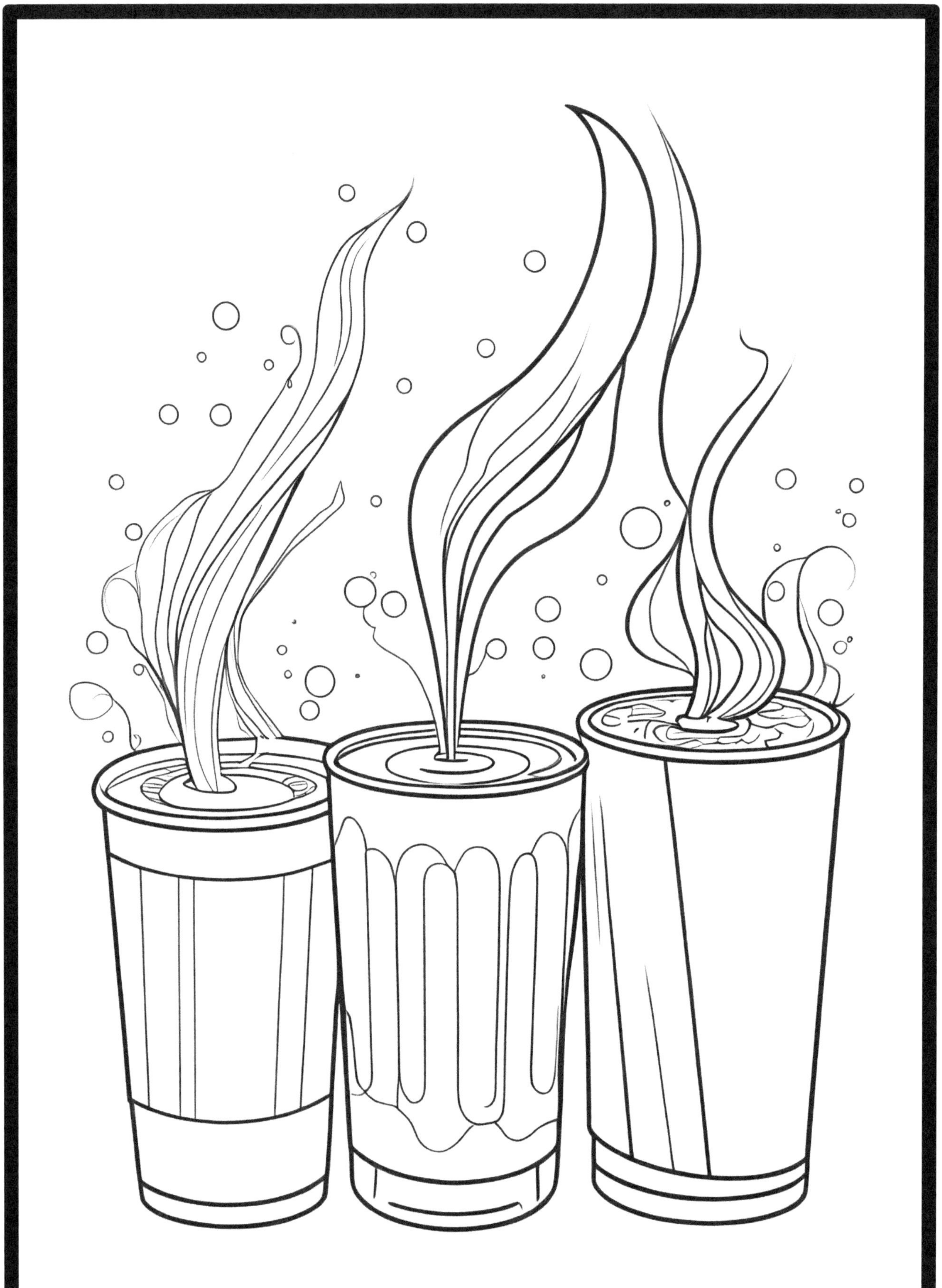

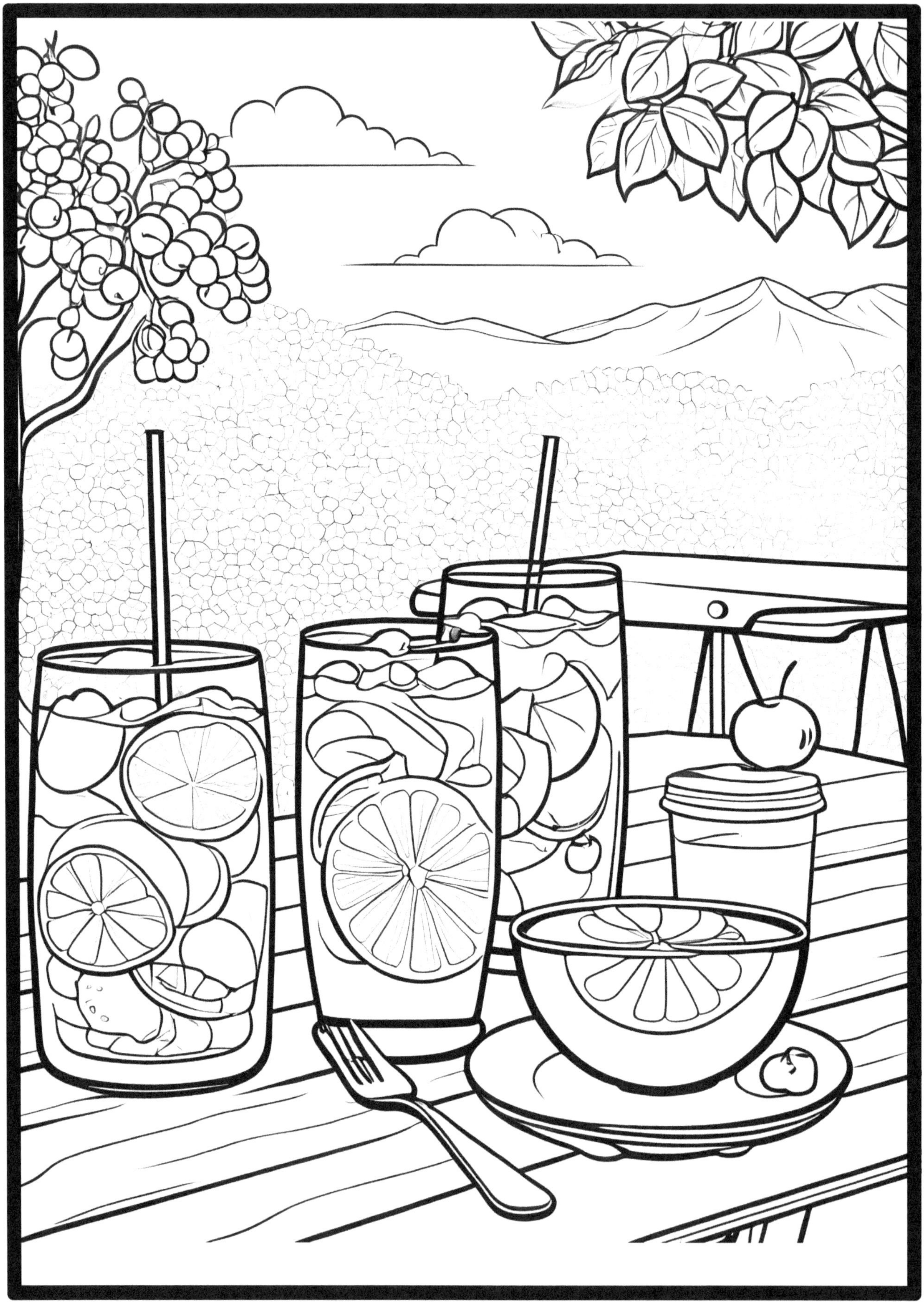

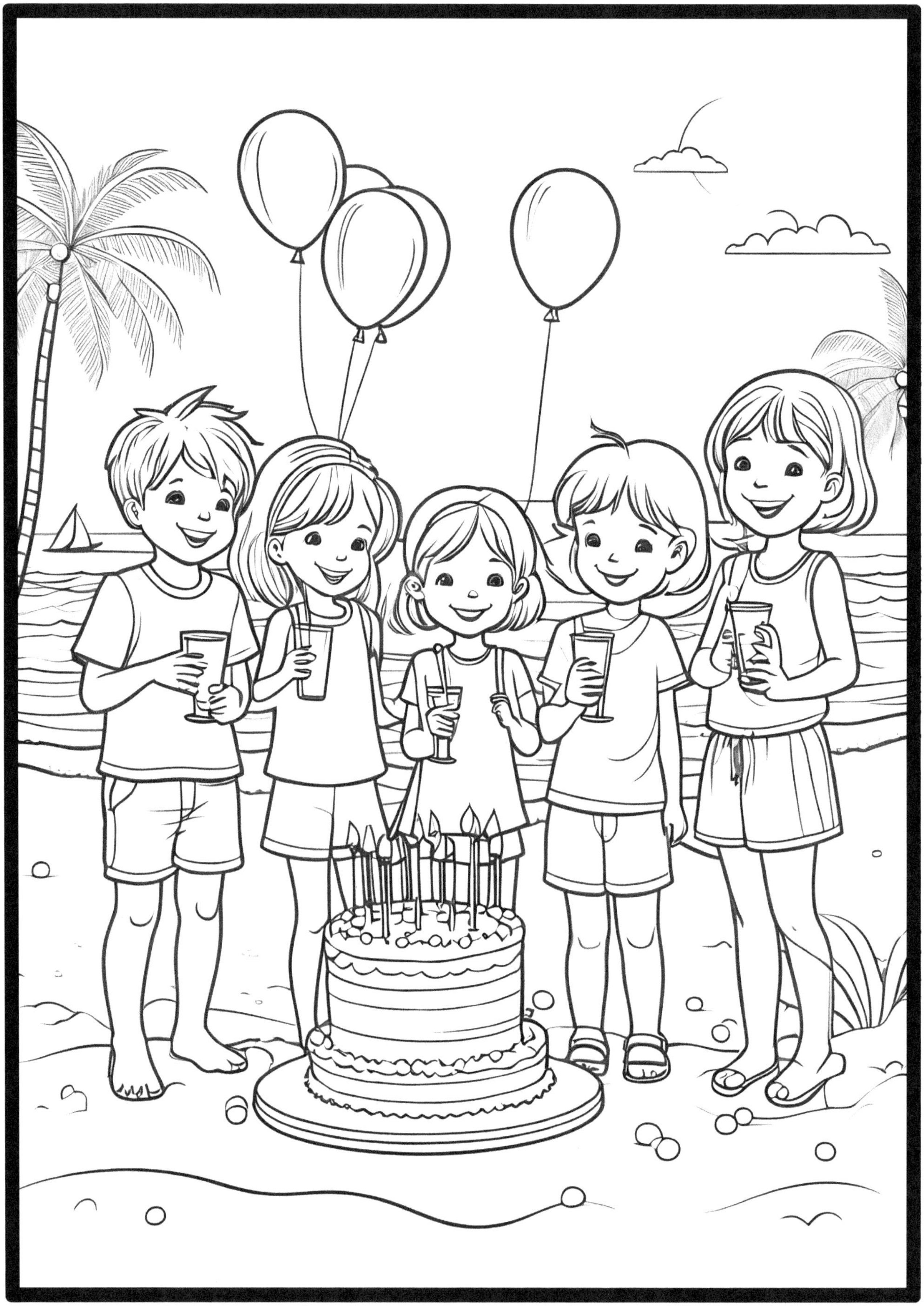

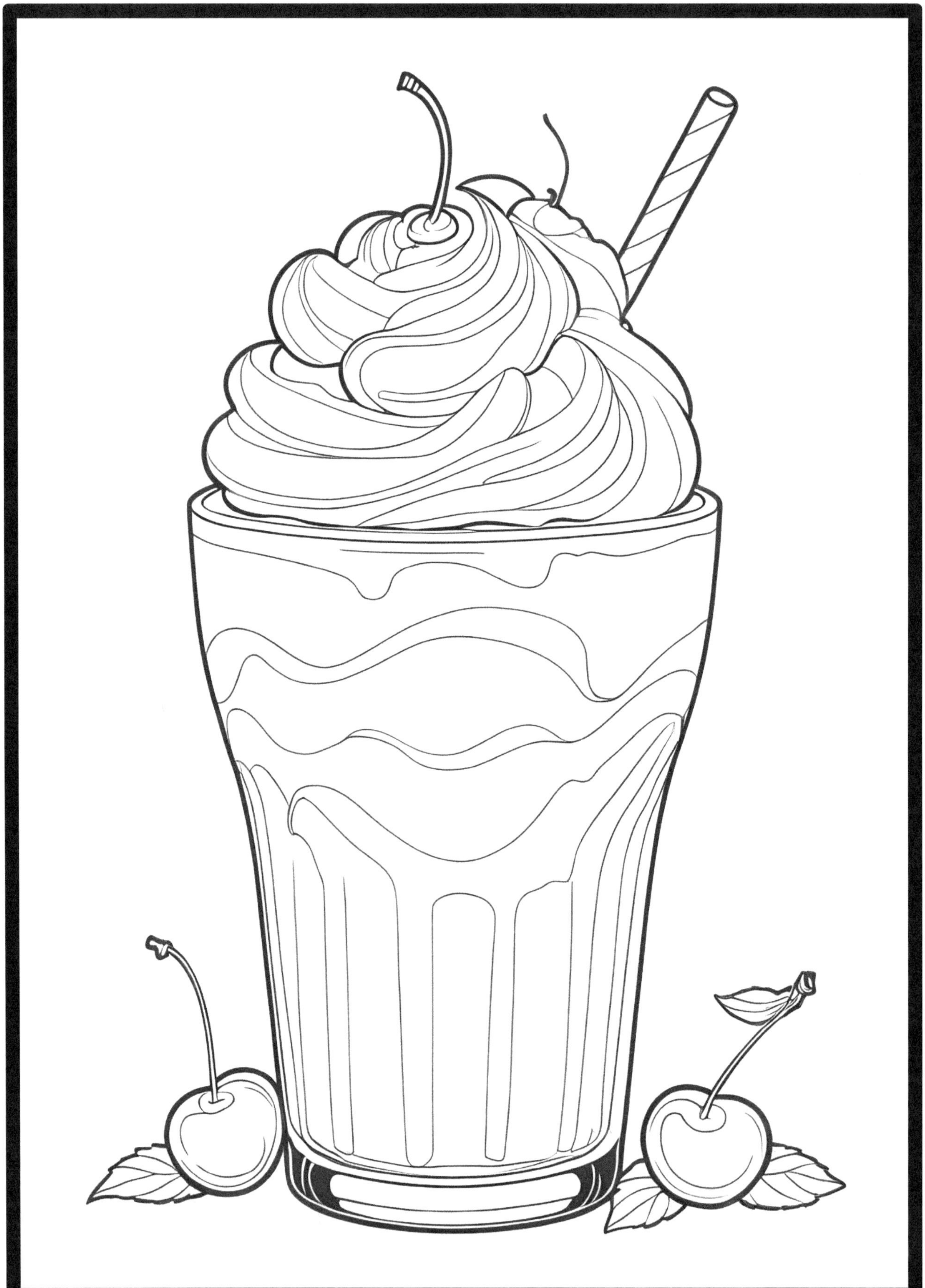

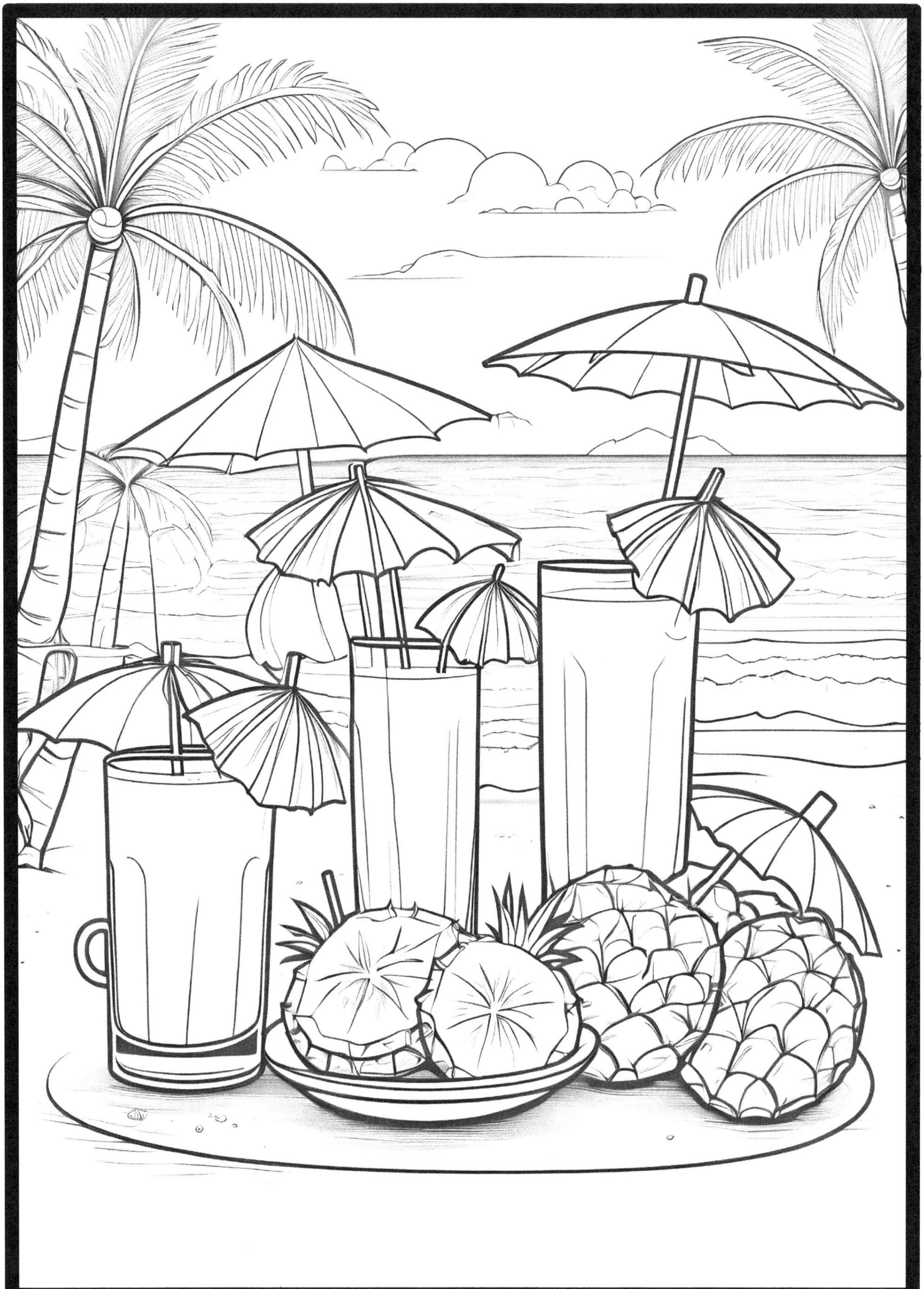

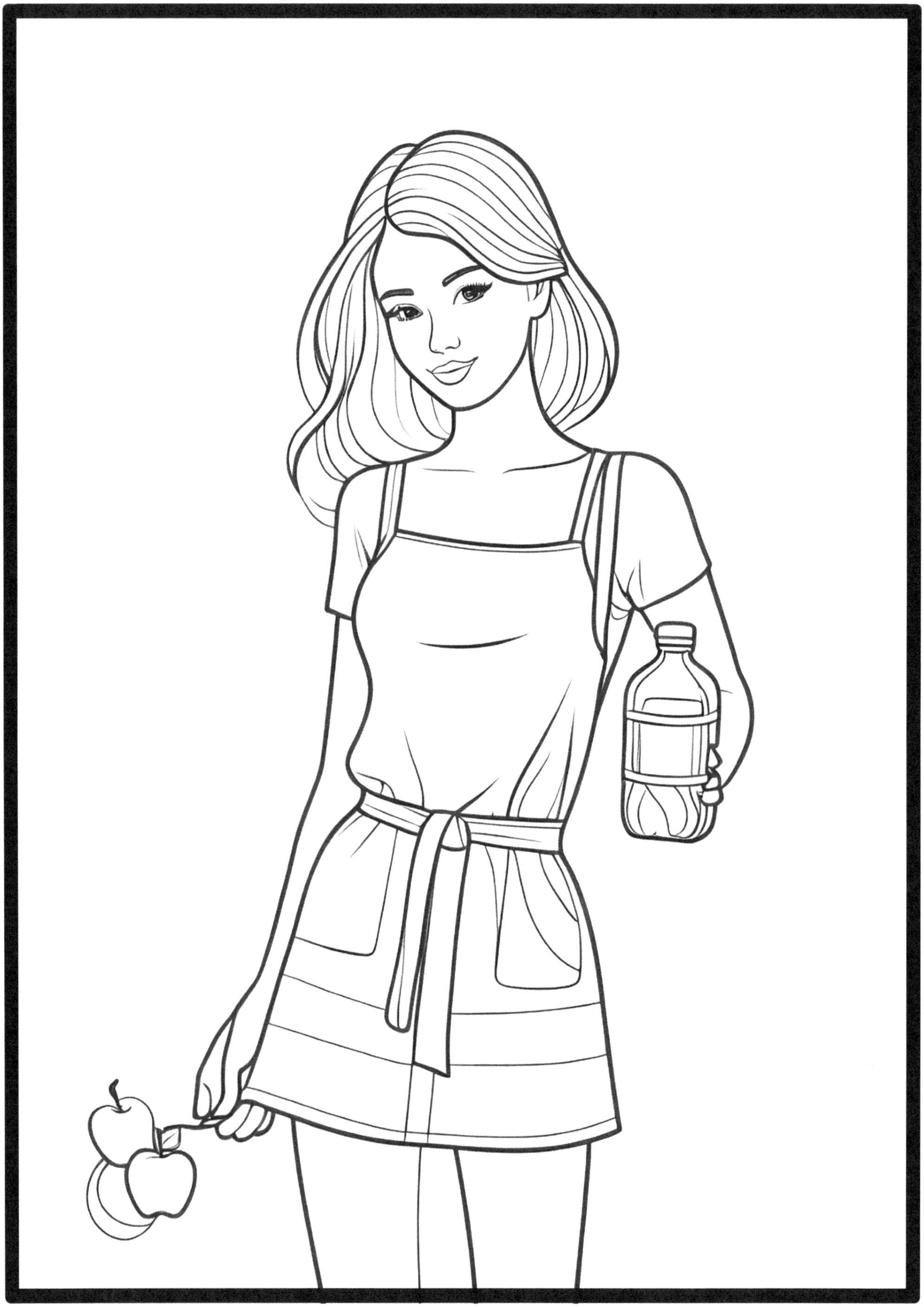

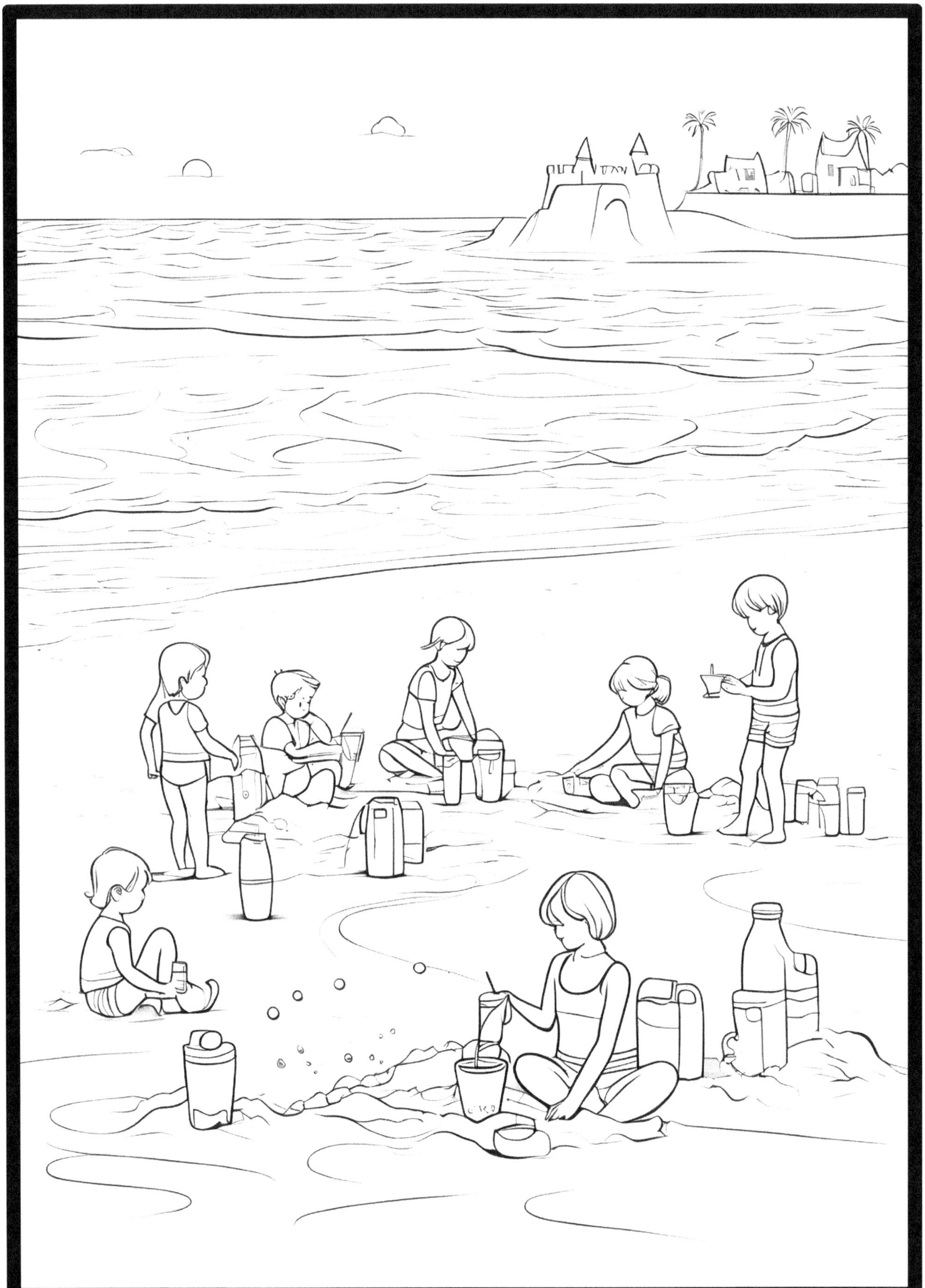

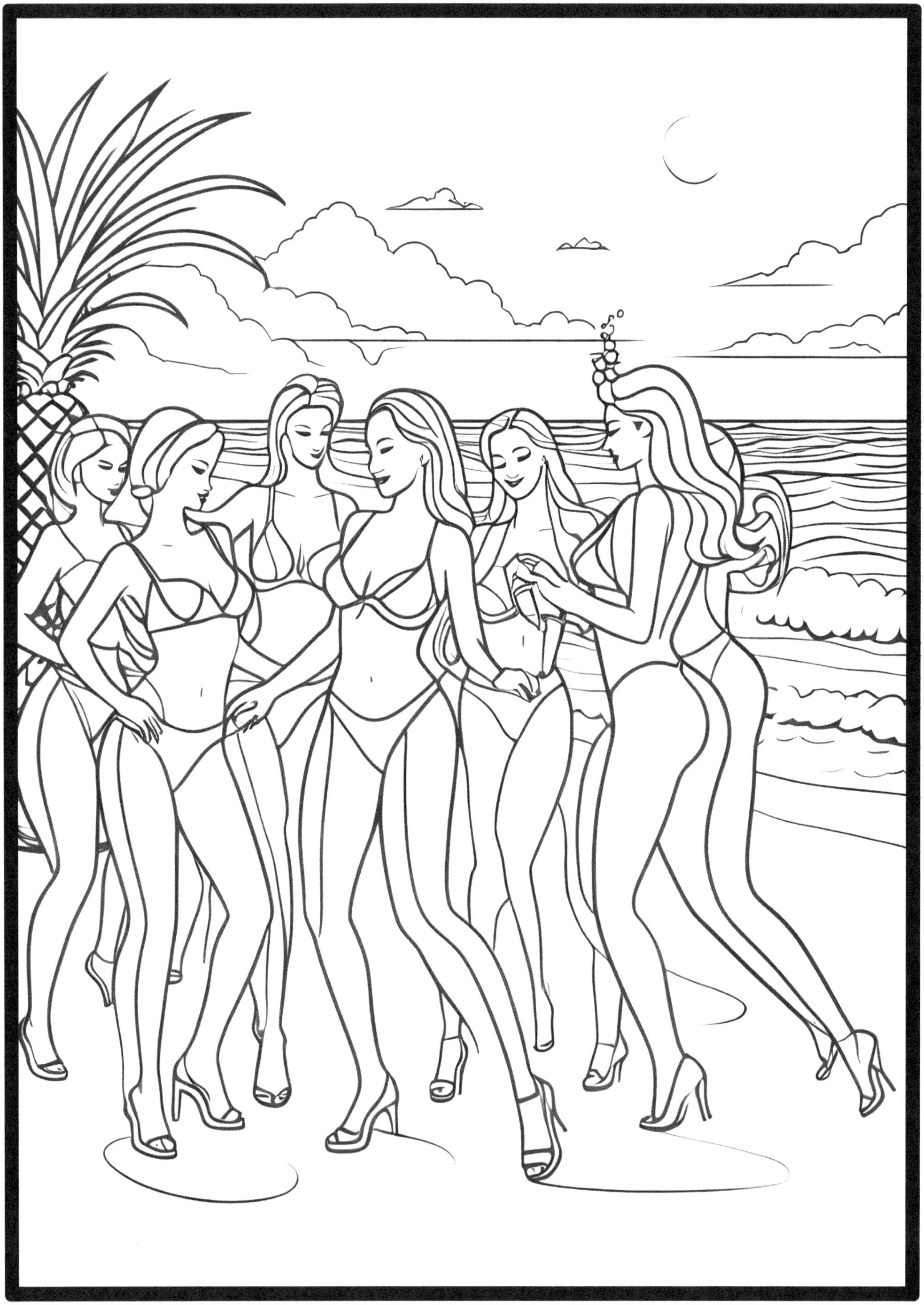

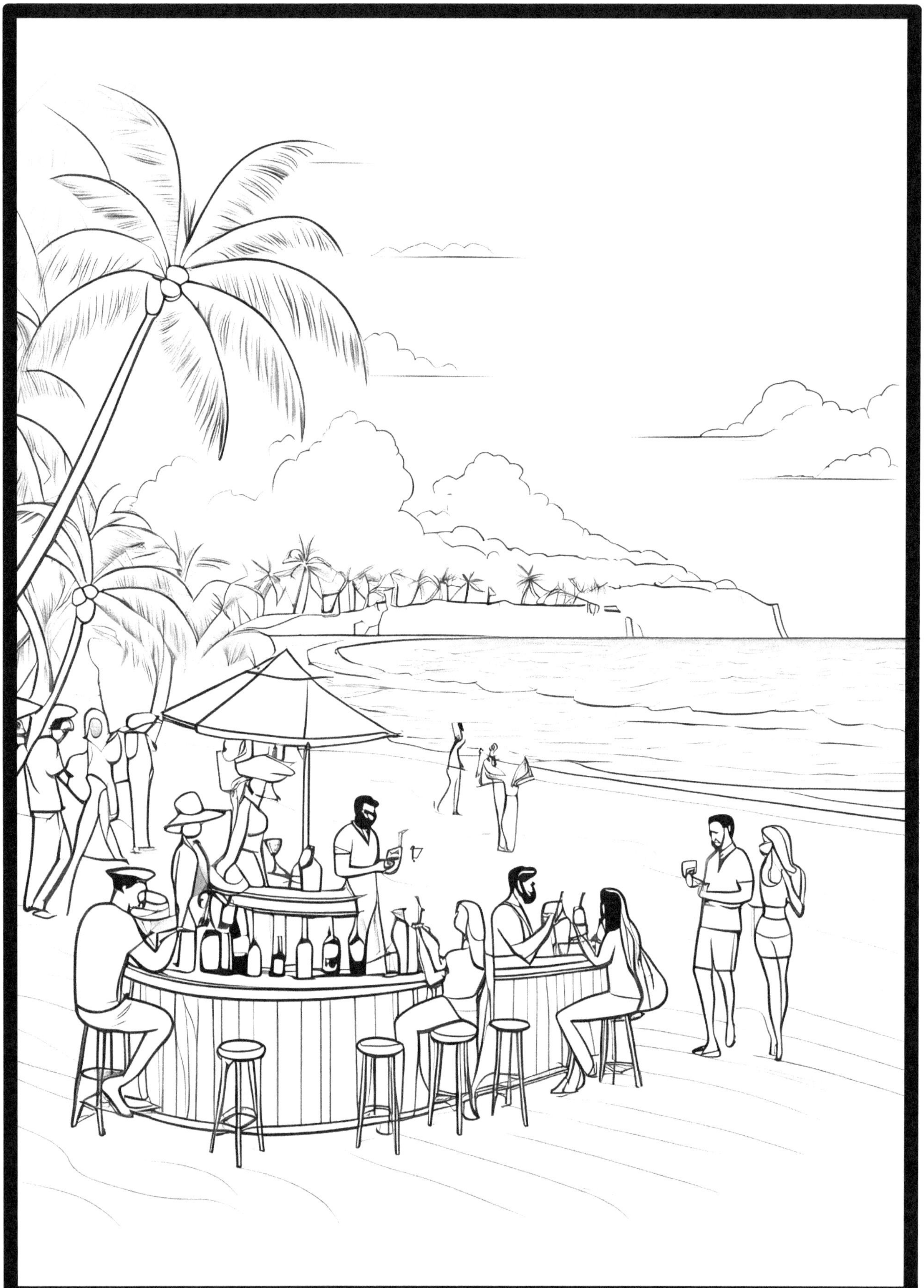

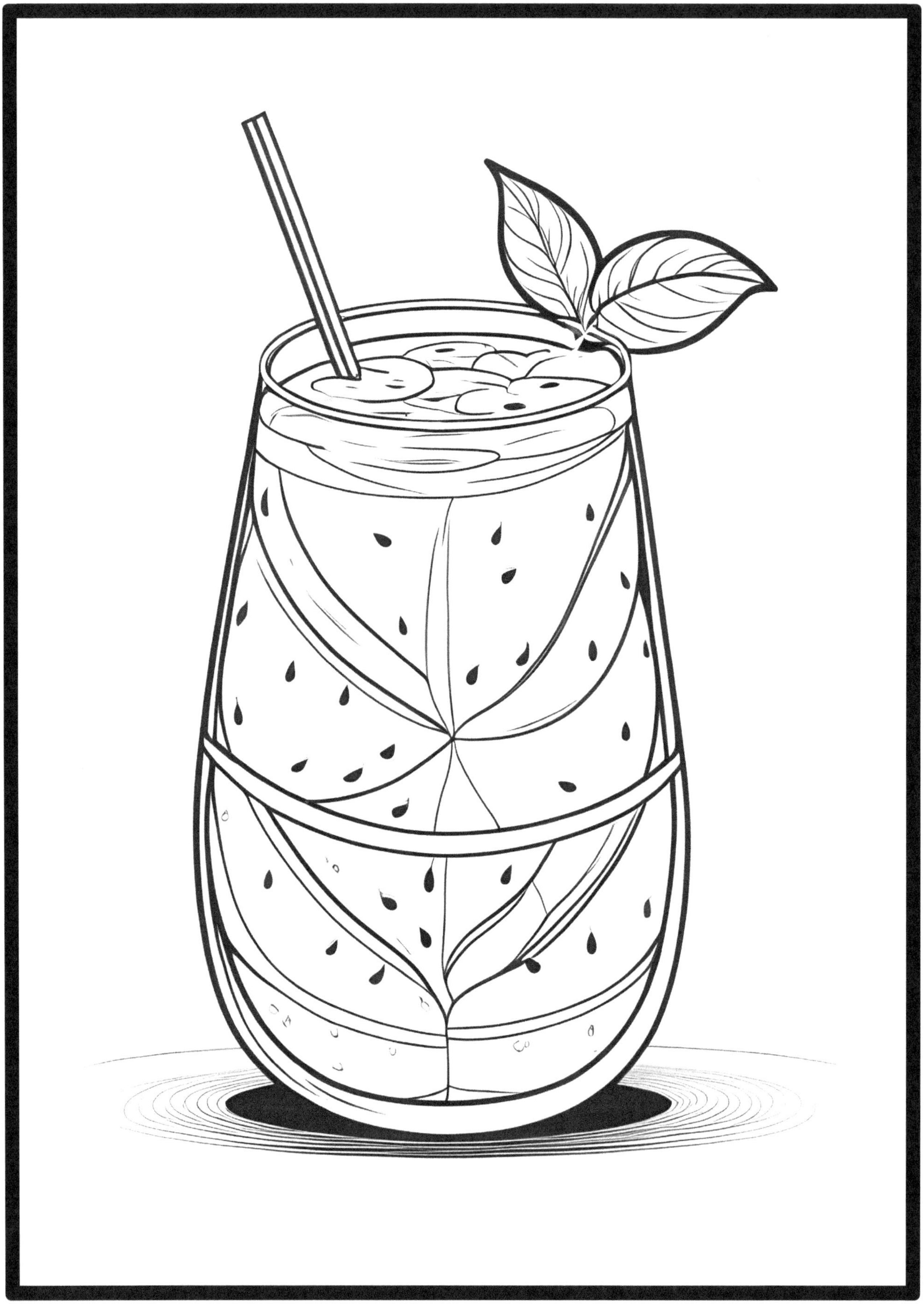

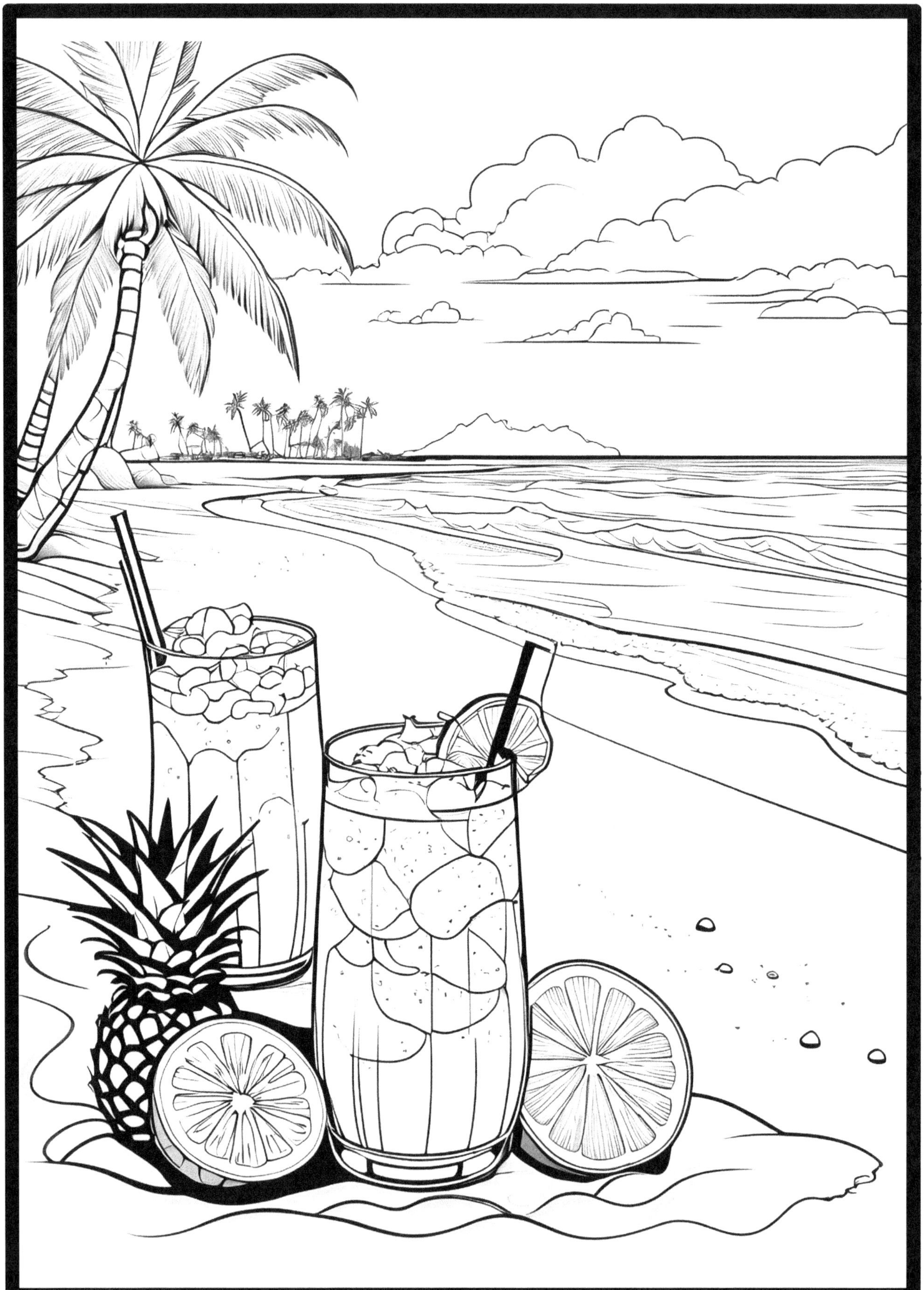

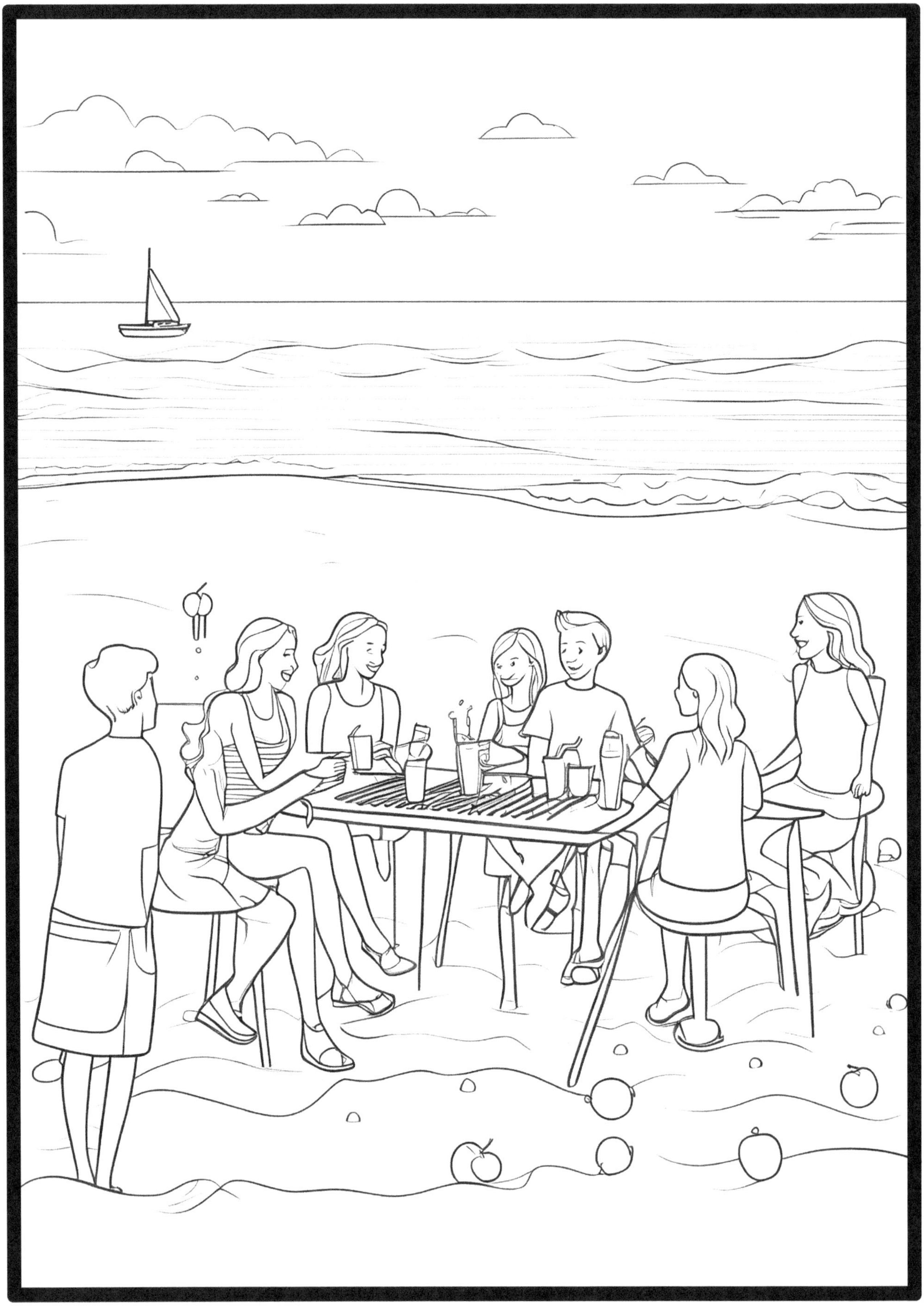

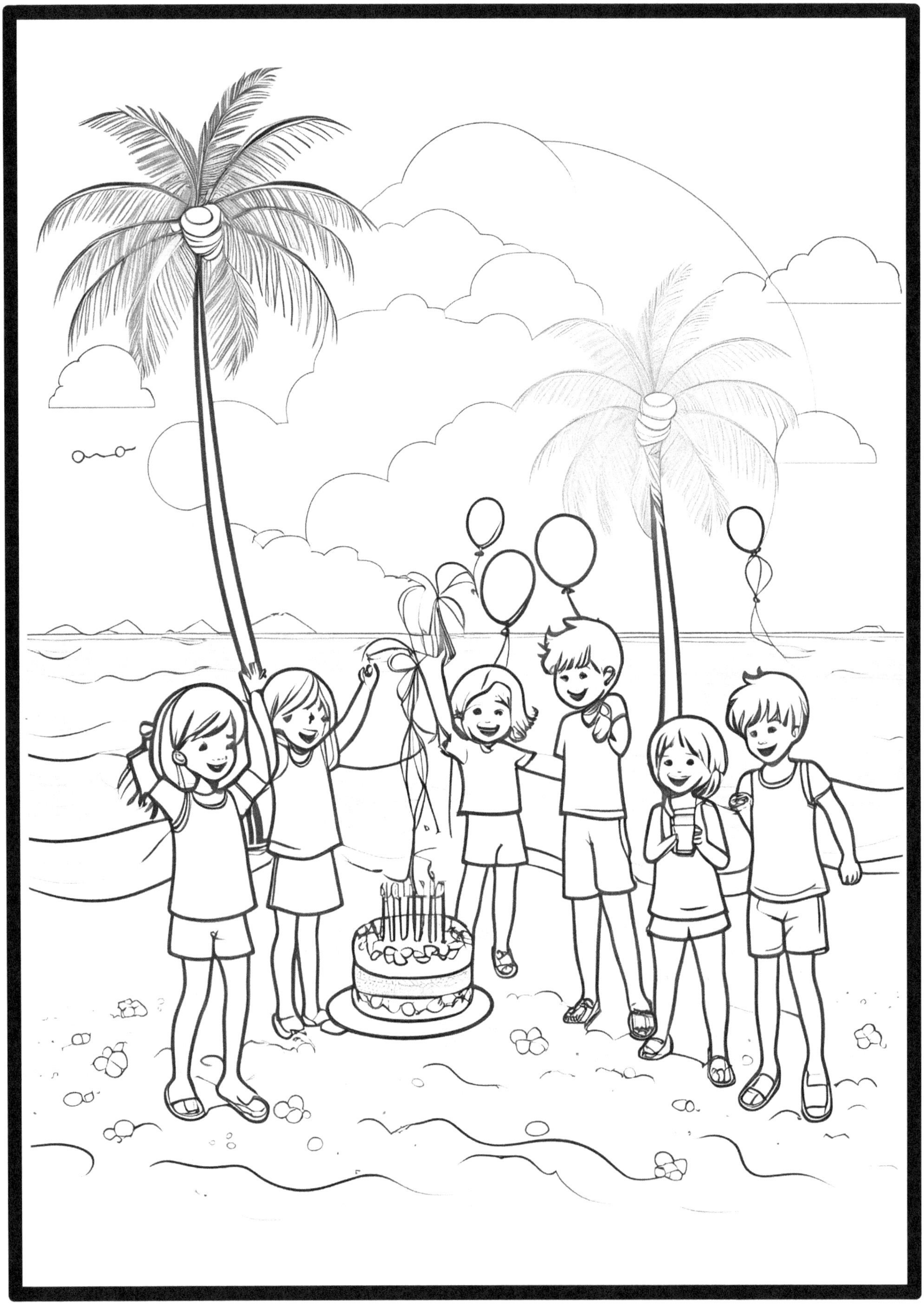

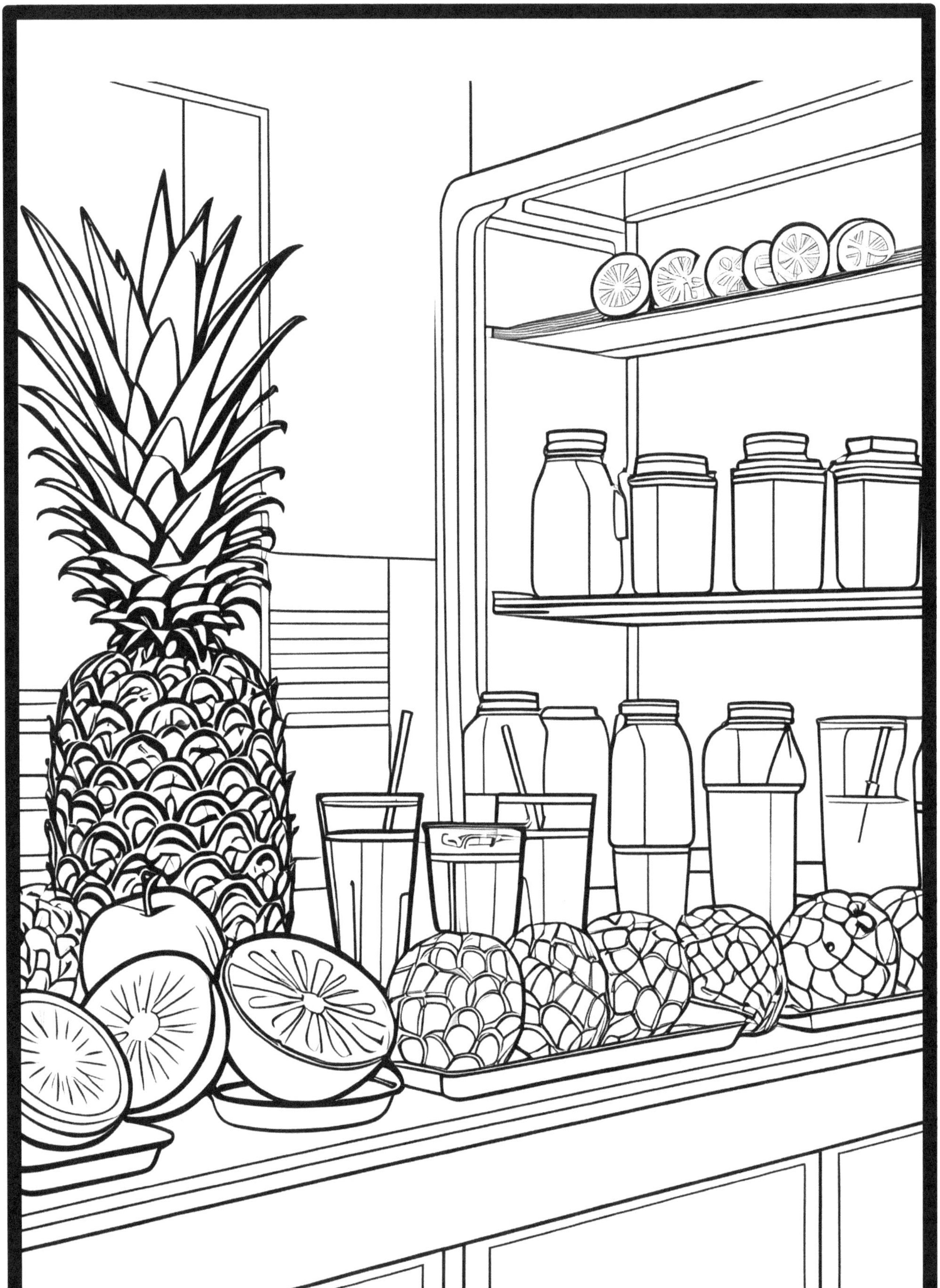

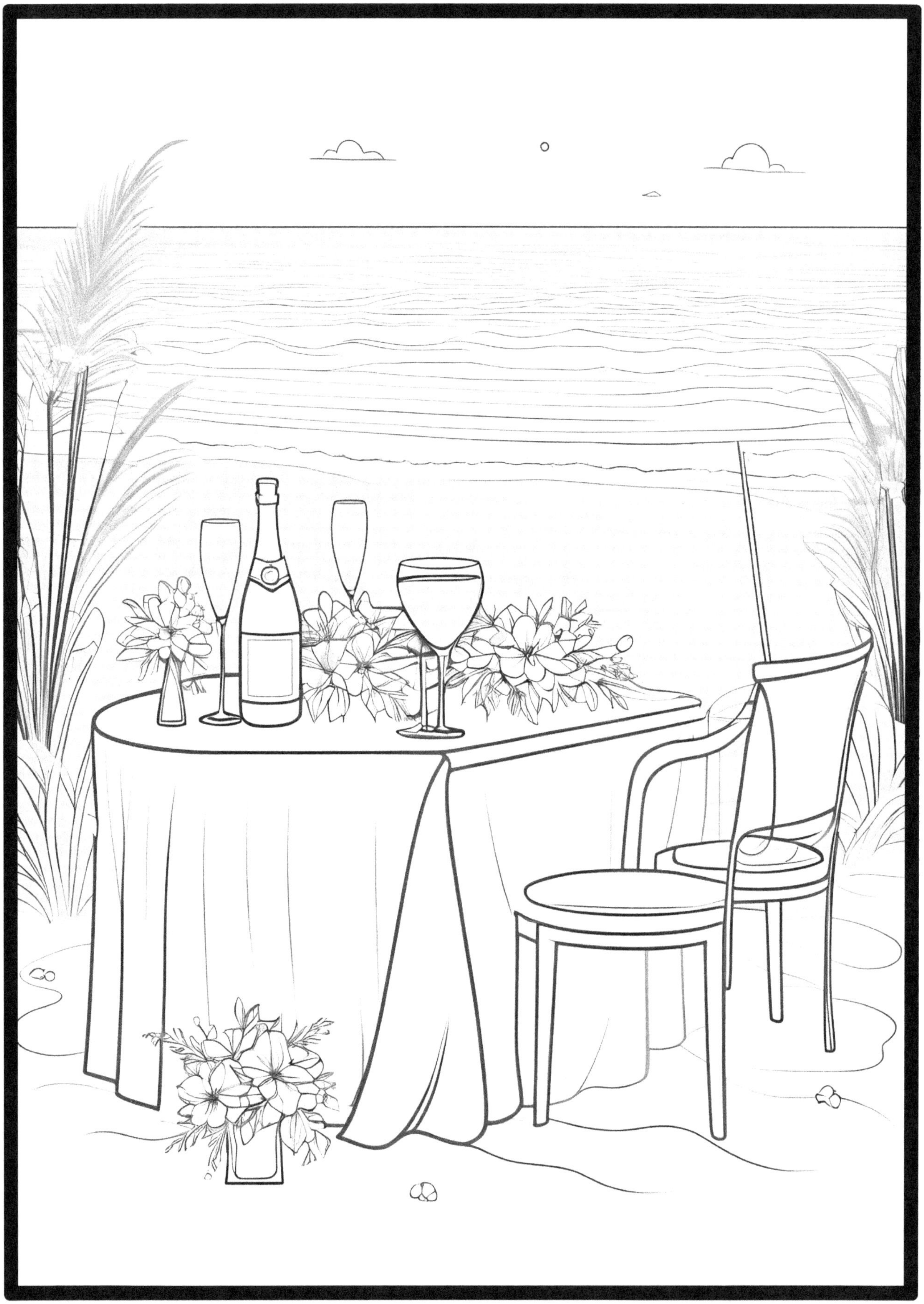

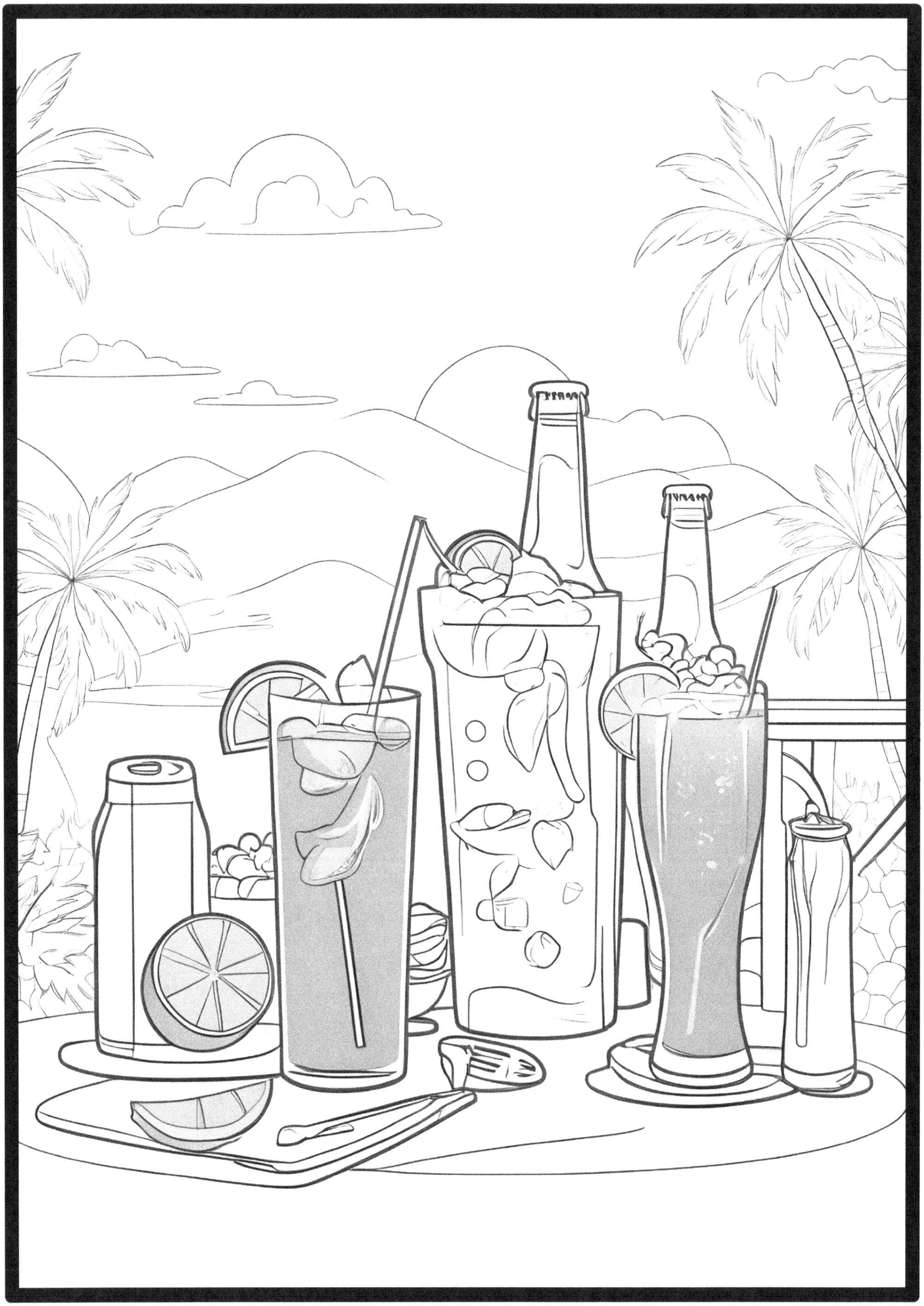

www.ingramcontent.com/pod-product-compliance
Lightning Source LLC
Chambersburg PA
CBHW062357220526
45472CB00008B/1839